Single-Minded

Being single, whole
and living life to the full

Kate Wharton

MONARCH
BOOKS

Oxford, UK & Grand Rapids, Michigan, USA

Published by Monarch Books
an imprint of
Lion Hudson plc
Wilkinson House, Jordan Hill Road,
Oxford OX2 8DR, England
Email: monarch@lionhudson.com
www.lionhudson.com/monarch

ISBN 978 0 85721 430 0
e-ISBN 978 0 85721 431 7

First edition 2013

Acknowledgments
Unless otherwise indicated, Scripture quotations taken from the
the Holy Bible, New International Version Anglicised. Copyright
© 1979, 1984, 2011 Biblica, formerly International Bible Society.
Used by permission of Hodder & Stoughton Ltd, an Hachette
UK company. All rights reserved. "NIV" is a registered trademark
of Biblica. UK trademark number 1448790. Scripture quotations
marked The Message taken from The Message. Copyright © by
Eugene H. Peterson 1993, 1994, 1995, 1996, 2000, 2001, 2002.
Used by permission of NavPress Publishing Group.

A catalogue record for this book is available from the British
Library

Printed and bound in the UK, May 2013, LH26

Contents

Chapter 1

Wholly single

Full life or half life?

Often it can feel as though being single is to be a "half" rather than a whole. Sometimes we see ourselves in that way, in our darker moments, when we feel lonely, and wish we had someone by our side with whom we could share life. Sometimes others see us in that way, and we feel judged by society for our singleness. When we have to fill in a form and tick a box marked "single"; when we have to pay a single room supplement for a holiday; when we are faced with "2 for 1" supermarket offers that we know we'll end up throwing away; when we steel ourselves to enter a party alone; when we need someone to hold the other piece of the flatpack furniture we're building; when we come home to an empty house and there is no one to tell about the highs and lows of our day – at these times, and at many others, being single can feel like the raw end of the deal.

But we are not half-people, we are whole people! We mustn't fall into the trap of seeing ourselves in this way, and we mustn't let anyone else do it either. Whether we are single or married; whether we have children or not; whether we live alone or with others – we are "whole". Each one of us is a whole, complete person, made in the image of God, to reflect his glory.

I conducted a wedding once where the couple had a poem read in the service which contained the line "We used to feel vaguely incomplete, now together we are whole".[1] I've also heard numerous pop songs and watched films that speak of being "made complete" when we finally find that special person to marry.

For some people, it seems as if perhaps marriage, or their spouse, or relationships in general, is their "god", since that is where they find their security. But unless we know our security and our identity to be firmly placed in God then we will never be truly happy or fulfilled.

Jesus said "I have come that they may have life, and have it to the full."[2] That is the life that we are offered in Jesus Christ. Full life. Complete life. Whole life. Not a life which will only be complete when we find the missing other half of ourselves. Life that is full and complete and whole right now *because* it is life in him. Our identity is found in Jesus. A full life is one where we don't miss out on any of what God has in store for us; where we make the most of every opportunity that he brings our way; where we spend as much time with him as we possibly can; where we seek to share his good news with as many people as we possibly can; where we are comfortable with who he has made us to be; where we are full of joy because of the amazing things he has done for us.

It's fairly common to hear people introduce their spouse or partner as "my other half". You're bound to have heard it. This is something we have to be careful with. At its heart, it's a biblical statement. In the creation account in Genesis we read that "a man leaves his father and mother and is united to his wife, and they become one flesh."[3] Therefore, when someone gets married they don't become in any way less themselves, but they do in a mysterious way become half of a whole unit.

At the same time, however, this can lead to those of us who aren't married feeling as if we are somehow less than whole. It can feel this way if we've never been married, because we may see ourselves as one half waiting for its other half in order to become complete (and it's not unusual to hear people actually talking in this kind of language). It can also feel this way if we've been married but are no longer – we may feel that our wholeness has been destroyed and we are back to being half a person. In both cases single people can end up feeling that by themselves they are only half a person – somehow unfinished.

Philippa is in her thirties and has always been single. She's part of a large church with a high proportion of single people, and the church is good at encouraging people to connect together in groups and support one another. She finds that where there are difficulties in understanding it tends to be between young families and single people, often because they don't spend enough time together to really understand one another's issues and concerns. She values the freedom being single gives her to be generous with time and money – being able to give a great deal to friends because there are no further demands waiting back at home. The difficulties she finds are when big things have been discussed at work that married people can go home to share with spouses, as she has no one with whom to share those things. She also feels that this is an area in which the church should invest more time and do more teaching – as a church we take care to prepare people for marriage, and we should do the same to prepare people for what may be a whole life lived as a single person.

Recently an article was published on the BBC News Magazine pages by a man describing his experience of being single. Tellingly, the article was entitled "Why are couples so mean to single people?" He considers the viewpoint that being single is to have somehow "failed", and reflects that, "You see, no one is supposed to be single. If we are, we must account for our deficiencies."[4]

The way we need to look at this is that as single people we are whole by ourselves – it's not true that we're incomplete unless or until we get married. We're children of God, made in his image and that's just the same whether we are single or married. However when two people get married, two whole people come together and a new "whole" is created – the marriage unit is greater than the sum of its parts.

I wonder whether you've ever been asked the question "Have you got a family?" I find that I get asked that quite a lot, especially when I'm being introduced to someone for the first time. If I'm feeling bolshy I might reply, "Yes I have – I've got a mum and dad, a grandma, five cousins…" , but if I haven't got the energy for it then I'll probably just weakly mutter "No, I haven't…" You see, what is really being asked is "Are you married with children?" In that question, family equals spouse and children. If you haven't got them, then the underlying assumption seems to be that you aren't a family, you haven't got a family, and all is somehow not quite right.

Maybe you've also been asked "So, are you still single?" with the emphasis on the "still" as though there's something a bit odd about you for not having had the decency to get yourself married yet. Sometimes we fall into the trap ourselves, and we might say that we're single "at the moment", as if we're somehow ashamed to admit it out loud. Our society, and even our churches, can sometimes seem to give the impression that when we "grow up" we should get married – that it's just one step in the journey of "normal" life. I've even heard people run those two quite separate life events together and talk to children about what they'll do when they "grow up and get married" – somehow seeming to infer that not doing the second of those things means that the first hasn't quite been achieved either.

And yet if we allow ourselves to think like that, and if we allow such stereotypes to go unchallenged, then it's all too easy to fall into the trap of seeing our single life as some sort of waiting room for when the "proper" life of marriage begins. I wonder if you recognize that sense of thinking your life will really begin when you meet that special someone whom you want to marry, and who wants to marry you. Maybe you're aware that at some point in your life you have felt like that, or maybe you would say that's how you feel right now.

Kerry is in her forties and has never married. She is very involved in her church and feels that there are people who understand some of the issues around being single, and ask about her life and work so she has someone to share with. Plus they give good hugs! However, many also think that being single she will have much more time than those who are married, and somehow be able to help with everything. She would also like it if they consciously thought more about the issues around singleness and sought to address them, rather than seeing it as a "phase". She has many married friends who welcome her into their family, help with practical tasks, and "appreciate me in my singleness and the gifts that that can bring". She enjoys the freedom and independence that singleness brings, in terms of how she spends her time and money, but is also aware of the things that she misses out on, such as sharing food and drink with another person, and having someone to share dreams and plans with.

Odd one out?

When I hear poems, songs or film lines like those mentioned earlier, or when I get asked one of those questions, or others like them, I feel a bit sad and a bit angry. I feel that way because of the assumption contained within them that all single people are just sort of flailing aimlessly around having a half-hearted attempt at living life, until they can be rescued by a marriage partner and made whole. It's clearly nonsense when it's put like that. It's an assumption that I'm sure those asking the questions wouldn't consciously wish to make. And yet how many of us actually live our lives in some way being shaped and influenced by that attitude?

And I don't think that it's completely our fault. Society – and unfortunately also the church – just sort of funnels us into thinking in that way. Very often it can feel to us as though everyone around us expects us to be paired off and part of a couple, and that maybe we're seen as just a little bit odd if that's not the case. And I think because of that we also can end up viewing marriage as "the norm" and can make it our goal, so we can easily fall into the trap of putting our lives on hold and constantly saying "When I get married I will…"

How many of us, I wonder, are in danger of putting our lives on hold until we get married? How many of us think "Well, I would like to travel to such and such a place," or "I would like to get involved with that ministry in church," or "I would like to go on a mission trip," or "I would like to buy a house" – or countless other thoughts and ideas – "but I can't do it on my own, so I'll wait until I'm married and then I'll do

27

it." Have you ever gone through that sort of thought process? It's really easy to do.

There was once an article in the *Daily Mail* where a single woman bemoaned the trials of food shopping for one. She said this: "Supermarkets are obviously designed by married people for married people. If you fancy some mangetout for your supper... you must buy enough for a week ... [Packs of vegetables] sit on the shelf glowering at you, society's silent reproach for your failure to find a partner." We can laugh at that, but actually, we've all been there, and it can sometimes feel a bit like a conspiracy. Even though on the one hand we read statistics which tell us that more and more people are staying single for longer, on the other hand the whole of society sometimes feels as though it functions only for couples. Another recent newspaper article claimed that "living alone costs singletons an extra £250,000 over a lifetime compared to couples." That seems like a huge figure, but it was based on statistics such as the relatively higher cost of council tax for someone living alone, the "meal for two" deals in supermarkets that aren't available in a "for one" version, and the fact that holidays tend to be more expensive for single people.

An interesting issue to consider here is the fact that being single doesn't mean the same for Christians as it does for other people. When Christians say single they mean unmarried, and therefore unattached and celibate. When non-Christians say single, they mean without a partner, and therefore free and available for all sorts of sexual encounters and complicated combinations of relationships. Journalist and TV presenter

Mariella Frostrup has described the single life as "solvency, great sex, and a guilt-free life".[5] So although non-Christian people might still choose to refer to themselves as single, they don't generally mean "unattached", and sometimes therefore they regard with suspicion those of us who are entirely unattached, and living and functioning, in general terms, "alone". And so we can sometimes find that society isn't set up for us, and that it doesn't quite know what to do with us.

Sadly, we can sometimes find that the same is true of the church. Church life often tends to be set up, at a default level, for people who are married, and also, in general, for people who are married and have children. Much of the language used in our churches is about "couples" or "families". Lots of churches have that wonderful thing called a "family service", which can feel exclusive to those of us who are not in the traditional and expected sense part of a "family". If people want to grow a church they'll often say, "What we need is some more young families". I've never once heard a church leader say, "What we could do with in our church is a few more single people". Instead we hear talk of "a couple needed to take over leading the home group," or "some families needed to commit to the new church plant," or "two or three couples needed to plan the weekend away". Those are all phrases I myself have heard. No doubt the intention was never to exclude single people – but that can be what is heard and felt. I wonder if those phrases, and others like them, sound familiar to you? We're going to think a bit more about the church's attitude to single people in chapter two.

Les is in his sixties and has never been married. He finds that his church is very family-oriented. He does have married friends who encourage and affirm him, but finds that he has to take the initiative in contacting them, and that, due to distance or circumstances, they are only really able to keep in touch by phone. He enjoys the freedom that comes from being single in terms of choosing how he uses his time; however, he describes the worst thing about being single as "loneliness, loneliness and loneliness!"

The big issues...

I've been grateful during the writing of this book for the numerous single people who have shared with me the highs and lows as they experience them, and who have allowed me to tell parts of their stories. One thing that I did was to list seven issues which I felt were relevant for single people, and to ask people to grade them on a scale of 1 to 10, where 1 indicated that it was hardly ever an issue, and 10 indicated that it was a very significant issue. I looked at each issue in turn and saw where it had been given a score of 7 or higher.

The issues came out in the following order:

Lack of touch	54%
Holidays	44%
Talking/sharing	39%
Loneliness	32%
Sex (i.e. not having it!)	24%

Childlessness	17%
Living alone	10%

It's very interesting to look at the results. Lack of touch was a significant issue for over half of the people who responded, and yet as Christians I would guess that we probably experience more safe, positive touch than those who are not Christians, since lots of churches have the practice of "sharing the peace" or at least greeting each other at some point with a handshake, hug or kiss. Holidays were a significant issue for almost half of the people who responded. I imagine this might be one that married people don't expect or are surprised by, and yet isn't it sad that something which is meant to be fun and relaxing can become such a cause of difficulty and stress?

The next two also scored quite highly – not having someone there to talk to and share with, and being lonely. I think these are probably the two where our church family, and our close friends, can help the most, by offering warm, loving, supportive friendships and by being there for us in the ups and downs of life.

The percentage of people who found living without sex a significant issue was lower than I expected (maybe they didn't feel able to be totally honest…?). However, I also wonder whether there is something here about the difference between simply not having sex, and living a pure life. We're going to look at this in more depth in chapters three and four, but I wonder whether the answer would have been different if I had asked who found it difficult to live a holy, chaste, celibate life.

Childlessness and living alone scored quite low marks because some people who responded had children, and quite a number did not live alone.

Unwanted gift?

We often hear the phrase "the gift of singleness" talked about in our churches, but what is it really all about? In author Al Hsu's book *The Single Issue* he writes a great paragraph about this. He says:

> No question makes singles more uneasy. And no concept generates more confusion for singles. "Ah, the gift of singleness," one single friend mused. "Sometimes I wonder if it's like a Christmas gift you want to return. You know, you get something from someone and you think, 'This is nice, but I'd rather have another sweater than this one.' Well I'd rather have the gift of marriage than the gift of singleness!"[6]

So what does the Bible say? Well it *doesn't* say, "If you have the gift of singleness, you will be perfectly happy to never get married." Paul uses the "gift" language in a chapter devoted to discussions of marriage and singleness. He says this: "I wish that all of you were as I am. But each of you has your own gift from God; one has this gift, another has that."[7] This is the only time that "gift" is used in this way, and it isn't expanded on, but traditionally the view has been that if you don't feel totally comfortable being single then you don't have the gift of singleness – regardless of whether or not you are actually single.

Al Hsu points out the flaws in this argument when applied instead to marriage – no married person wonders, "Hmm, do I really have the gift of marriage or not?" They can't conclude that they don't have the gift and decide to leave their marriage. Instead they have to get on with doing the best job of being married that they can. And so it is with those of us who are single, and have to do the best job that we can to live well within our current circumstances. And of course, on one day that might feel perfectly fine and straightforward, yet the next day it might feel like a terrible burden and struggle.

There is also an implication in the traditional view of the gift of singleness that if we have the gift then we should be free from all sexual desire, but we do not find this argument anywhere in the Bible. I think it is incredibly helpful at this point to recognize and understand that Jesus was "tempted in every way, just as we are – yet he did not sin."[8] And if this is true, if Jesus' identification with us is going to mean anything at all, then it must also be true to say that he was tempted by sexual sin, just as he was tempted by many other sins. Of course he never committed any sin, but he was tempted, and so he understands and identifies with our temptations, yet he shows us a model of how to resist temptation and live with holiness and purity.

The idea of a "gift" is an interesting one to unpack as we think about what it might mean. If we replace the word "gift" with "grace", then perhaps we can think not about a "gift of singleness", but instead about "grace for singleness". This sounds much more appealing to me! It also strikes me as much more practically useful. God gives us grace for whatever situation we currently find ourselves in. This analogy also works when we make a comparison with marriage – most of our churches would make a high priority of preparing people for marriage, praying for people who are married, and encouraging people to put effort and energy into making marriage work. Yet we don't treat singleness in the same way. Maybe we should all think and pray more about the "grace" which is required in order to live the single life well.

The point is that there is no two-tier system of singleness whereby some super-holy people are called to a permanent state of singleness and miraculously equipped to live in it, while others must simply struggle on through. Some people, such as those in religious orders, are of course called to live a single life forever. It is not necessarily the case, however, that at the same time as they are called, their wish to be married and their sexual desires are removed or replaced.

There is no need for a special gift in order to endure the supposed horrors of a single life. These are false and unhelpful attitudes which we must steer clear of and deflect when they come our way. Instead, we must do our best to find the secret, as Paul did, of being, "content whatever the circumstances"[9] – whether married or single.

It is also fairly obviously unhelpful to state that if someone doesn't have the gift of singleness then they should get married. The response here is likely to be "I would if I could!" It's just not as easy as that. If we are currently single then we have the "gift" of singleness – that is simply our current state of being. We will retain that gift unless we get married, in which case we will exchange it for the "gift" of marriage. Both good, both different. Simple as that. How freeing it is to read and understand it in that way! We are free to try to live a full and whole life as a single person, desiring and pursuing marriage if we wish, but not seeing it as a step-up from where we currently are. And marriage doesn't mean the end of the single life forever. When a marriage breaks down, or when one partner dies, people find themselves single again, and a process of readjustment is needed.

We also need to beware of the viewpoint that says there is one perfect person in the world for us and that just as soon as we find them it will all be OK. This is a common idea, which seems romantic and appealing, and it's often the way life seems to work in the movies! However, in the real world I don't think this is how it is. We don't have just one soulmate in the world with whom we will fit perfectly together. If we take this view we are in danger of getting angry and frustrated with God, and of storing up bitterness, as we will blame him for our single state and wonder why he hasn't enabled us to meet "the one" for us.

Let's not fall into the trap of seeing all this purely in negative terms. It is of course true that for some people being single is a difficult and painful thing, but for others it is a positive and enjoyable thing. And for most of us, perhaps, it is sometimes good and sometimes bad; sometimes freeing and sometimes lonely; sometimes a blessing and sometimes a source of great pain – and those feelings will change from week to week, day to day, even hour to hour! And even if we do find it painful, and would prefer to be married, we do nevertheless have to continue to live our lives day by day, so it is important to look for, be grateful for, and embrace the positives which are undoubtedly part of this way of life.

Caroline is in her sixties and has never been married. She feels that her church understands some of the issues she faces as single person, like the fact that there is only her to do all the chores around the house. Some members also offer her practical help on occasions if they recognize a need. She feels that there are financial advantages to being single, and enjoys the freedom to do what she wants with her time. However, she finds that it's harder to create a social life outside of work as a single person, since you have to take more of the initiative yourself. It can also be harder to take time off work, as single people aren't seen to "need" as much time off as those with families do. She feels that a lot of the issues to do with being single which were very difficult when she was younger have become easier as time has gone on, since she has become used to living with them.

Who am I?

Hold on a moment though – if we are in danger of finding ourselves swept along on a tide of "coupledom" and feeling like the odd one out for being single, then we need to find a corrective that restores our equilibrium and reminds us of what is really true and what is not. Generally the best place to turn to when we need such a corrective is the Bible!

Psalm 139 is a beautiful and well-known psalm about identity – about who we are before God, about how he made us, why he made us, and what he wants for our lives. This is how it reads in The Message version:

> Oh yes, you shaped me first inside, then out;
> you formed me in my mother's womb.
> I thank you, High God—you're breathtaking!
> Body and soul, I am marvellously made!
> I worship in adoration—what a creation!
> You know me inside and out,
> you know every bone in my body;
> you know exactly how I was made, bit by bit,
> how I was sculpted from nothing into something.
> Like an open book, you watched me grow from
> conception to birth;
> all the stages of my life were spread out before you,
> The days of my life all prepared
> before I'd even lived one day."[10]

Did you read those words as relating to you? That's how God made YOU. You are marvellously made, by him, to be you.

37

He didn't make you to be anyone else, and he didn't make you like some jigsaw piece that needs to find another piece before it is finished. You are whole and complete just as you are. You're not made to be alone, admittedly – none of us are. The Bible tells us that quite clearly, as the first time God said that anything was "not good" was when he was talking about Adam being alone.[11] But "must not be alone" is not the same as "must be married". The problem that God says is "not good" is loneliness. One solution to this is marriage, but it is not the only solution. We need friendships and relationships, certainly, to both enhance and enrich our lives, and in order to love and serve others, but we need no one else in order to be a whole and complete human being.

Life to the full

The apostle Paul says this: "For in Christ all the fullness of the Deity lives in bodily form, and in Christ you have been brought to fullness."[12] All the fullness of God lives in us, and we have been brought to fullness in him. Not to half-ness, or almost-completeness, but fullness. So often the message that we are given from the world around us is that we cannot be happy and complete and fulfilled by ourselves. That is a wrong message to begin with.

The idea that if we can only find ourselves a partner, any partner, then we will be happy and complete and fulfilled is also wrong. Some single people seem to believe this to be the case, and anticipate that all of their problems and issues will miraculously disappear on their wedding day. They put on their rose-tinted glasses and dream of how much better their life will be after they are married. But of course any issues we have as a single person will still remain once we are married – and they will be brought into even sharper focus as we find ourselves suddenly face to face with another human being, having to learn to co-exist in a whole new way! Marriage is a wonderful thing, but it also involves a huge cost, as a promise is made from that point on to put someone else's needs ahead of your own.

In the book *Boy Meets Girl*, Joshua Harris reflects that some single people want to ask when their turn for marriage will come. He replies like this:

> If you're single, I believe that God wants you to see
> that your story *has* begun. Life doesn't start when
> you find a spouse. Marriage is wonderful, but it's
> simply a new chapter in life. It's just a new way to
> do what we're all created to do – to live for and
> glorify our Creator.[13]

We need to find happiness, contentment, and fulfillment within our own individual lives – we cannot and will not find them with another person. And those things can only come from a life that is totally surrendered to God.

Whether it's waiting to decorate our house, or to move house, or to buy a new car, or to start a new job, or to go back to studying, or to travel abroad, or to go on a mission trip, or to do any of the things we considered earlier in the chapter, we don't need to put our plans on hold – we can do them now!

Sometimes we can find ourselves feeling paralysed in the face of the big decisions in life, and feel that they are too big for us to make on our own. We tell ourselves that we will do them, one day, when we are married and we have a partner to do them with. But why wait? If we do end up getting married we want to have some life experiences to share together, not just a blank and empty life because we've been waiting for that moment before we start anything. And if we don't, we want to have had some great experiences as we go through life. I know it can be hard to make these big decisions by ourselves, but we can do it – we don't have to wait.

And it's the same with the smaller things in our lives. We can opt out of going to see that new film we like the look of, or trying that new restaurant, or starting that new hobby. We tell ourselves that all those things will be more fun once we have a partner, and so we wait. But why not do them now? For some of them, we can gather a group of other single people and do them together. For others, we can go along with our married friends. And for some we can just dive in and do them by ourselves. The first time you go out for a meal in a restaurant by yourself, with a book to read, and order a glass of wine, you might feel self-conscious – as though everyone is watching. The chances are they haven't noticed and are too busy having a good time themselves. But even if they have noticed, who cares? They are probably envious of your self-confidence and freedom anyway! So why not give it a go?

Some of these things might feel lonely to do by ourselves, but some will feel fantastic! I love going to the cinema by myself – it's not as if you can talk when the film is on anyway.

I please myself about what I want to see, and where I want to sit, and I don't have to share my popcorn with anyone else. I don't want to end up in ten years with a list of movies I wish I'd seen but didn't because I didn't have anyone to go with.

Mandy is in her fifties and is divorced. She finds her church is supportive of her but feels that this is "as a person" rather than as a single person. There isn't any particular teaching on singleness – she thinks that this is to do with the subject just not being quite as "on the radar" as other subjects are, and also that singleness can be seen as a "transition period" rather than as a longer-term state. She values her married friends who look out for her and check that she's OK. She doesn't like the fact that some people assume she is unfulfilled as a single person and that she would like to get married again, whereas in fact she is very happy as she is. She notes that it takes some discipline for single people who live alone to take any time out for themselves – with no one there to urge you to stop working, there's a tendency to just keep going.

To turn to another assumption I often hear, I think it's a myth that single people have more free time than married people with children. Nevertheless, I think it is true to say that we have a different sort of availability with our time. For instance, we are far more able to make spontaneous decisions, such as deciding to go on holiday the following week, or responding to a party invitation for that evening. We only have ourselves to worry about and we can make whatever plans we choose. The flip side of this, of course, is that there is only one of us to do all the jobs that need to be done! Paul, writing to the church in Corinth, says this: "The time and energy that married people spend on caring for and nurturing each other, the unmarried can spend in becoming whole and holy instruments of God."[14] I love that – let's make an effort to become whole and holy for God!

As single people we are able to enjoy a huge amount of freedom. This covers everything from choosing to turn off the phone and watch our favourite movies all day long on our day off, to decorating our house however we choose, to deciding where to go on holiday, to eating whatever we like for dinner. We can choose to take a new job, move house, travel abroad, begin a new ministry. I'm not saying it is easy to make these decisions and do these things on our own – but we do have incredible freedom to choose. I have travelled a lot over the past ten years or so, and it's one of my favourite things to do, but I am well aware that I've been able to do things and go to places that I might not otherwise have been able to had I had a family to consider. Of course, big decisions such as these need to be made prayerfully, and in line with what we believe God is calling us to do (whether married or single). Nevertheless, single people have a different type of freedom and opportunity with regard to such decisions.

We also have a huge opportunity in terms of witnessing to friends, colleagues, family members, and neighbours. People notice how we live. They notice if the things we say don't match up with the things we do. They notice the decisions we make, and the reasons we give for having made them. They notice how we deal with the tough times. They notice where our focus lies and what our priorities are. This is perhaps especially true in this area of sex and relationships, when choosing to live a pure, holy, celibate life is very countercultural. I've occasionally had people make fun of me for the way I've chosen to live, but without fail that has led into conversations about why I've made those choices, and about the things that are most important in my life. When we live lives that are whole and complete, with God at the centre, it is a powerful witness.

Another thing I think we can very clearly see as a positive is the opportunity that we have for intimacy with God. Now of course God should be the number one priority for all Christians. However, it is true that when people have a spouse or children they have other people to whom they need to give very high priority. Obviously I'm not saying that married people or parents don't love God as much as single people! But I do find that lots of my married friends are envious of the opportunities I have to really be deeply intimate with Jesus, to see him as my best friend, my brother, my lover, and my husband. Instead of first being someone's spouse or parent, I can choose first to be a follower of Jesus. And it is my choice whether or not I make the most of that opportunity. I can choose to invest everything I have in that relationship and earnestly desire all that God has for me.

We need to remember that solitude (as opposed to loneliness) can be received and enjoyed as a positive thing.

43

Lots of my friends who have children look back wistfully to the days when they could have a quiet time (or let's face it, even go to the toilet!) without a small person tugging at their leg and demanding attention. We have the opportunity to be alone with God, to pray, to go on retreat, and to make a choice to turn potential times of loneliness into times of solitude and blessing. I'm not saying it's easy, but it is about making a positive choice.

The challenges and the issues will be slightly different for each of us. The things I find difficult won't be the same as the things you find difficult, and the strategies I use to cope won't be the same as the strategies you use to cope. What you need to try to do is to work out what's good and bad for you, what helps and what hurts, what works and what doesn't.

There will be different issues for people who have been married but who have become single again, whether following divorce or the death of a spouse. There may be many regrets there. We'll look at that in more detail in chapter five. But again you can't allow yourself to be ruled by those feelings of regret, and fail to make the most of the rest of your life.

I'm not saying there won't be times when it's difficult and painful, because there will. There are those times in everyone's life, no matter what their life circumstances are. But we only have one opportunity to live an earthly life, and it's a precious gift that we've been given from God, so let's grasp it, and really live it.

In Luke's Gospel we read these words:

"Truly I tell you," Jesus said to them, "no one who has left home or wife or brothers or sisters or parents or children for the sake of the kingdom of God will fail to receive many times as much in this age, and in the age to come eternal life."[15]

These words can encourage us not to have regrets about what we haven't got, but instead to focus on what we have got in this life, as well – and so importantly – as on what we will one day receive. For Christians, our perspective is beyond this life to the life to come, the life which is promised to those who know and love God. In the final book of the Bible, Revelation, we read about a vision of the new heaven and new earth:

Look! God's dwelling place is now among the people, and he will dwell with them. They will be his people, and God himself will be with them and be their God. "He will wipe every tear from their eyes. There will be no more death" or mourning or crying or pain, for the old order of things has passed away.[16]

Keeping our eyes fixed on this future reminds us of the hope and promise we have in Jesus.

In Eric and Leslie Ludy's book *When God Writes Your Love Story*, they describe a time when Eric's sister Krissy was asked whether she felt she was called to singleness. She paused for a moment before replying, "Today I am."[17] That's a beautiful, balanced response, isn't it?

The old hymn "Great is Thy Faithfulness" contains the line "Strength for today and bright hope for tomorrow".[18] I think that sums up pretty well what we need to live this life – strength to live our lives for God, honouring him in everything we do; and hope to enable us to keep going day after day, knowing that God is always with us.

Shane Claiborne is involved in something called The Simple Way, a Christian community in Philadelphia, and he's written lots of books. He's an amazing guy. He was interviewed recently in *Christianity* magazine. At the time of the interview he was single. This is what he said:

> I think we have a lot to learn about the gift of singleness to the Church and for the sake of the gospel. Jesus talks about it in Matthew. Paul talks about it. You look at folks like Mother Teresa and you don't think, "Oh, man, if only she had met her husband." Part of what allowed her to be the sort of witness that she was, was her singleness and her single-minded devotion to God. One of my mentors is a monk, and he says, "We have to realise that in our society we're obsessed with sex, but our deepest longing is not for sex but for love. We can live without sex, but we can't live without love." We have to figure out how to create communities where people can love and be loved, and then I think that other questions around sexuality get a bit easier.
>
> I've dated a few people over the last decade, and the question that I'm always asking is: "Are

we more, together, than we are on our own for God?" I think what I have certainly learned from the monastic renewals in the church is that "mono" means single, it's the single-minded pursuit of God, as the pearl we leave everything for; it's the love that we say "no" to all other lovers for. The real question is: "How can I pursue God with the most single-mindedness and the least distractions?" That's what I'll continue to ask.[19]

For us as single people, I think that is our great challenge – to develop the "single-minded devotion to God" that Claiborne identifies in Mother Teresa. That should be what we are known for, first and foremost. And when we fully devote ourselves to God in this way, we will discover that the "full life" that Jesus came to bring is available to us all – we can be wholly single.

Chapter 2

Living a God-obsessed life in a marriage-obsessed church

I wonder, what did you think when you first saw the title of this chapter? What do I mean when I talk about a "marriage-obsessed" church? Is that an unfair description? Or is it only too real and true? I have some wonderful, kind, understanding married friends within the church; however, I also know that I have had my fair share of crass and insensitive comments from married Christians with regard to the issue of singleness. If you've been single for any length of time, then I'm sure you have had such comments too!

My favourite example is a time when I was taking a funeral. Just before it started, the funeral director (who is a Christian, and who I knew a bit but not very well) began to engage me in conversation. He asked me out of the blue whether I had a boyfriend and, a bit taken aback, I replied that I didn't. He knew that I would soon be moving on to a new church and so he said that I would have to make sure that my new church had lots of single men in it. I decided to make a joke of it (rather than shoving him into the empty grave next to us, as I was tempted to do), so I laughed and said, "Well, if you hear of any churches like that do let me know, won't you?" To which he said, I kid you not, "Well you'd better get a move on, you don't want to leave it too late." I couldn't believe it! I half expected him to do a sort of *Countdown* clock thing with his arm and go "Tick tock, tick tock"!

I'm sure he didn't mean to be hurtful, but conversations such as that one, and other similar ones I have had (and I'm sure you have too!), are very interesting, aren't they? If we are being charitable, we might say that the reason married Christians ask us about our relationship status, and comment upon it, is that they are happily married, so they rightly see marriage as a wonderful thing. Naturally they would like everyone else to be as happy as they are, and often they assume that being married is what everyone wants. And that reasoning may work for people that we know well and who genuinely care for us and are interested in our lives. But with people we barely know, what on earth makes them think they have permission to speak so frankly about such a personal area of our lives?

I think it comes down to the way in which marriage and singleness are thought about, talked about, and valued in the church today. From my own experience and observations, as well as from numerous conversations with other single people of all ages, backgrounds, and denominations, my conclusion is that the church in the UK today seems to value marriage far above singleness. This often serves to make many single people feel that they are unable to have a full and active role within their churches or even, sadly, to feel like a full and valued member of their church family.

Gemma is in her forties. She's been part of different churches that have varied in how supportive they have been of her as a single person. She finds it more helpful when everyone mingles and joins in together, rather than when married and single people separate out into homogenous groups. She has also valued times (which have seemed rare!) when the person preaching has taken care not to describe married life as the ideal. She has also valued opportunities to be real in church – to be able to say when life is difficult and things are painful, whether in the area of singleness or in any other part of life. For Gemma the main issue is a lack of real companionship – "I feel I don't have anyone to share life with at a committed level." She also feels that married people often don't really understand some of the challenges and struggles of being single, and can (albeit unwittingly) say things which can be painful.

Back to basics

If we're going to begin to answer the question as to why this is, we need to look first at what the Bible and the church have to say about marriage and singleness.

We need to go right back to the beginning. When we do that we see, as mentioned in chapter one, that when Adam was created, God said "It is not good for the man to be alone. I will make a helper suitable for him."[1] This was the first time in the whole creation story that God had said, "It is *not* good." So God makes Eve as a helper for Adam. This isn't the place to get into an in-depth study of Genesis, but let's just be clear that "helper" doesn't mean skivvy, or in any way denote an inferior person. In fact, this same word is used elsewhere of God himself. What we really need to notice at this point is what God doesn't say. He does *not* say, "It is not good for the man to be single. I will make a wife suitable for him." What he *does* say is that what is not good is loneliness, aloneness; and that is what God remedies by creating Eve and all the people who come after them. So, as human beings we are made to live in community, in relationship, rather than totally on our own. Of course, this is also the moment at which the pattern of marriage between a man and a woman is established. From the beginning, God created community – married couples and single people, young and old, male and female, to live, work, and worship together.

The whole of Old Testament Israelite society was based on family clans. Marriage and children were at the heart of it all. There was no real place for single people within that society. Being single or childless meant that there would be no one to care for you in your old age. For a woman to be unable to bear children carried a huge social stigma. Having an heir was hugely important so that property could be handed on. We see the pain of women in the Old Testament such as Sarah, Rebekah, Rachel, Jephthah's daughter, Hannah and others, due to singleness or barrenness.

Although this was the prevailing view of the society at that time, God promised never to forget these women. In Isaiah we read these words:

> "'Sing, barren woman,
> you who never bore a child;
> burst into song, shout for joy,
> you who were never in labour;
> because more are the children of the
>   desolate woman
> than of her who has a husband,' says the Lord."[2]

The message we find throughout the whole of the Bible is that God is for those who are marginalized by their society. During times when unmarried or barren women were shunned, God spoke these words to bring them dignity and comfort.

The view of marriage being the norm continued, and it was still the prevailing world view in Jesus' day. It was required of Jewish men that they marry and have children. But in this area, as in so many others, Jesus was not afraid to turn the prevailing world view upside down. He taught that salvation comes from knowing him, not from marriage. He taught that eternal life comes from knowing him, not from having heirs to continue the family name. He taught that dignity and identity come from knowing him, not from any human relationship. And he created a new family, a new community – the church. Jesus called the people in this new church his brothers and sisters and mother, rather than those to whom he was biologically related.

Jesus also taught that marriage is an earthly state not an

eternal one, and that it will not exist in the new heavens and new earth. Sometimes we forget that at their wedding couples make a vow which will last "till death us do part". In the new heavens and new earth we will all be single!

In short, Jesus made it perfectly clear that following him was the most important thing that anyone could ever do – far more important than having a marriage partner or children. That's not to deny the importance of those things for people who have them, or to say that they aren't worthy and valuable. But what Jesus does is to radically alter the priorities which were accepted at that time, and to give new status and dignity to those who are single. In Luke's Gospel Jesus spoke to the crowds gathered around him and said, "If anyone comes to me and does not hate father and mother, wife and children, brothers and sisters – yes, even their own life – such a person cannot be my disciple."[3] The required priority in our lives is clear – Jesus must come first.

When Jesus speaks about eunuchs he makes it clear that both married and single people are equally able to serve God as whole and complete individuals.[4] And of course the mere fact that Jesus himself was single was a radical thing. He was respected as a teacher and a prophet, and yet he was an unmarried man, which would previously have been unthinkable. Jesus lived his life as part of a community of people, men and women – he travelled with them, talked with them, ate with them, and prayed with them.

Paul, too, spoke highly of the single life. He affirmed both marriage and singleness, but nevertheless expressed his admiration for the single life, and his desire that more people would remain single, like him.[5] He described the benefits of singleness in terms of being able to be fully committed to the work of the gospel. And he himself was another role model, a man living a full and complete life, respected as a teacher and leader.

The author Al Hsu, in his book *The Single Issue*, puts it like this, "Without demeaning marriage, the New Testament gives a new dignity to singleness. Both are equally valid ways to serve God."[6]

In the first few centuries of the early church, celibacy was recommended and promoted as the best way of life for serving God. This stood in contrast to the prevailing view of the rest of society at that time, which continued to highly value marriage. There were some within the church who went as far as denigrating marriage and declaring sex to be unclean. Celibacy became customary for clergy. Sometimes this was seen as a purely nominal thing, with some clergy engaging in illicit sexual relationships. When the Reformation took place, the Reformers sought to renew and cleanse the church and to restore its biblical roots. It was recognized that the requirement for clergy to remain unmarried was not scriptural. Marriage began to be encouraged once again among Protestant clergy, so that they were not seen as "set apart" from other Christians. We can see that at this time another shift began, back to seeing marriage as the better, purer state.

I would suggest that that is still the way in which much of the church in the UK currently functions, at least at a default level. Of course each one of us will have had different experiences, but I think it's still true to say that the majority of churches, to a greater or lesser extent, and implicitly or explicitly, seem to value marriage over and above singleness. They also, perhaps unintentionally, often seem to treat people who have never married as if they are in some kind of necessary but unpleasant limbo state prior to marriage. When I speak to single people from a huge variety and breadth of different churches, time and time again this seems to be their experience. Again, Al Hsu speaks wisdom here when he says that "A truly Christian view of both singleness and marriage will honour both equally without disparaging one or the other. Recovering such a balance is the first step towards a church where singles are valued equally with marrieds."[7]

Churches can be difficult places for single people to be, and yet surely this is all wrong! Church should be the place where everyone is welcomed, and where everyone is valued for who they are. Church should be the place where we all feel part of the family and where we all have something to contribute.

So what are some of the things that can go wrong, and that can lead to single people feeling as though they are not fully part of life in our churches?

I mentioned in my story at the beginning of this chapter that sometimes people can say things that are hurtful or insensitive but which are not meant in this way. In chapter six we're going to think a bit more about how married people and single people can "live together" – how they can get along as brothers and sisters, value and appreciate one another's gifts, and also love and support one another in the different life circumstances in which they find themselves.

Debbie is in her thirties and has never been married. She values being part of a Christian community with people in the same stage of life as her – younger single people. This means that it feels more of a supportive place for her than some previous churches have been, where she felt as though people were unsure of how to treat her. She finds that some of her married friends assume she is desperate to get married and would like them to pray for her to find a husband – she feels that this "colludes with the idea that if you're single you're somehow incomplete". She enjoys the spontaneity that is possible for single people in terms of making decisions, travelling, and so on. She feels that as a single person she might be more inclined to rely on God, as there are fewer alternative options available to her. She also talks about God teaching her to rest in the prayers and practical help of others in her Christian community, which is part of the way God provides practical help and support. However, she recognizes the danger of becoming selfish and set in her ways as a single person.

They're single, they love to serve

The first issue for single people in churches, I think, is one that can arise when they seek to serve in some area of their church's ministry.

My own experience, which seems to be borne out by others that I've spoken to, is that with regard to serving in church ministries, there are two equal and opposite problems that can occur.

One problem is the idea that single people have much more time than married people and are therefore always free to serve. Often this leads to single people being asked to do all sorts of jobs, far more than a married person would be asked to do. Single people might also be asked to help out at very short notice, with the implication being that they're bound to be free. This is a tricky one, because at one level of course we do have more time (if, that is, we don't have children, which of course isn't the case for all single people – this will be looked at more closely in chapter five). If we are single and without children, then we may initially appear to have more free time in the sense that we're not trying to juggle the demands of a spouse and children, and trying to find time to spend with them and to care for them. But the flip side to this is of course that there is only one of us, and all the same jobs – the cooking, cleaning, shopping, and so on – must still be done, and, assuming that we live on our own, then we are the ones who must do it! In addition, we need to bear in mind that when we want to socialize we often have to travel to see friends, and it soon becomes clear that the idea that "single people have more time" is a false one.

At this point I should say that the phrase above – "they're single, they love to serve" – is based on a sentence that somebody actually said to a class full of theological college students learning about marriage preparation. It was their response to whether single people could also be involved. They felt that yes, single people could certainly be involved, since they would have hours of free time on their hands waiting to be filled and would be happy to do any job at all because… well, you get the idea.

But the opposite problem, and something that I know is often an issue for single people, is that sometimes churches can treat us as if we are not quite "grown up" yet, and can be reluctant to let single people lead areas of ministry. Someone was recently talking to me about a particular church with a vacancy for a church leader and this person said to me – to me! – "They really need a good couple to go and lead that church." So I couldn't lead it? And not only that, but neither could Paul, nor Jesus? Often what people want in a church leader is some kind of "buy one, get one free" deal – they pay for the church leader and expect a hard-working spouse to be provided into the bargain. When the church leader is single (or of course, where the spouse doesn't want to or isn't able to fulfil this role), sometimes the church congregation can feel that they have missed out in some way.

I have heard from single people who have had this experience with regard to leading children's or youth work, or house groups. Married couples are asked to lead and single people who may be just as gifted, if not more so, are passed over with the implication that once they have "grown up and got married" then they will be able to lead too. Sometimes it is assumed that single people will want to do the children's work, perhaps because if they don't have their own children they will enjoy being with them, or because people who do have children want a break. At one level that's understandable, but at the end of the day, if you have the kids, you also have the responsibility to look after them! If a single person wants to do children's work that's great, but it shouldn't be assumed.

Perhaps the two problems I've outlined here are both extremes and exaggerations, but I certainly know of people who have experienced them both. We need to encourage our churches to walk the middle ground. Just as I believe that men and women are both equally able to serve and to lead in all areas of church life regardless of gender, so I believe that married and single people should also be able to be involved in whatever area of church ministry fits their gifts and skills, and to which they are called. We can get into all sorts of traps and stereotypes here. Women are better at children's work than men. People with children are better at children's work than people without children. Younger people are better at youth work than older people. Married people are better at leading house groups than single people. These are huge generalizations and they are, for the most part, nonsense! We each have our own unique set of gifts, skills, and interests, and we are each called by God to exercise them in different ways – that's what should determine where we serve, and nothing else.

Hayley is in her thirties. She was engaged in her twenties but the relationship broke down. She appreciates married friends who invite her to social events and ensure she is invited for Christmas and other special occasions. However, she finds that people often assume she has more time as a single person, so she can end up being asked to do more work, or being expected to finish things more quickly. The thing she finds hardest is seeing friends get married and have children, as this is something she would love for herself.

Loneliness vs solitude

The second issue that can arise for single people in churches is the issue of loneliness. It is often identified in surveys as being the biggest issue for single people, most especially, of course, for those who live alone. I do know that it is possible to feel lonely even in a crowd, and I'm sure that many people experience loneliness in a marriage where all is not well, but for single people I think this is a really big issue. And this is where community, and especially our church communities, can make a massive difference. At their best, our churches should work like families, where we all rub along together – old and young, married and single – and all love, support, cherish, and care for one another.

I wonder, is this something you can relate to? Do you often feel lonely? Although this can be a hard issue, if this is a problem and we want it to change, then it may be that we need to be proactive. The first step is to talk to people – friends, your small group, your church leader. Let them know that this is an issue for you. It might feel like a hard thing to do but perhaps they just don't realize, and they are more than likely to be keen to help once they're made aware of it.

Maybe someone could think about setting up a group for singles in your church, or if not a group just for singles, then at least for those roughly in your age group, for socializing and support. You could initiate a routine of having a meal together after church, or going to the pub together after the evening service, or meeting for a cup of tea one afternoon during the week. If you would like to be invited round to people's houses for meals but are not being, then why not take the initiative, and invite them round to your house instead?

If you don't currently serve in any ministry in your church, then why not start? Approach one of your church leaders and discuss with them what areas need help and where you think your gifts lie. You'll meet new people and feel more connected with your church family.

"You just don't get it"

The third issue I think single people can face is a general lack of understanding of their lives and their situations.

Leslie Ludy, in her book *Sacred Singleness*, says that single Christians "come to church hoping to find love, support and encouragement, but often the very people who should be cheering them on in their life of abandonment to Christ are the ones who overlook or disregard them because they are not married yet."[8]

Church should be the one place where we can be sure of finding love, acceptance, and support. It should be the place where we can take our pain and struggles and find people to love us through them and to pray for us in them. And our fellow Christians, our brothers and sisters in Christ, are surely the very people we ought to be able to rely on to love us unconditionally for who we are, not for who we would be if we were only paired off, and to allow us to be part of the same Christian family as them.

I know that I am fortunate to have some truly wonderful married Christian friends whom I love and who love me. There are a few of them who just really get it. Some of them are people of my age who are married and have children, and some of them don't have children. Some of them are older and have children who are grown up. But what they have in common is that they have allowed me to somehow become a part of their family. I can just hang out at their house, make myself feel at home, and help myself to a cup of tea when I want one. I can do things with them where it doesn't feel awkward that we are an odd number, and I don't feel like they have only invited me out of pity. They include me in family events, celebrations, and special times. They understand that there are times when I don't want to be on my own, and times when I do. They allow me to have a role in their children's lives. They rarely ask those stupid, insensitive questions, and if they do, I can tell them, and they apologize, and we laugh about it. They see me as a whole person, not a half waiting to become a whole. And I love them for it, and I am truly grateful to God for them.

However, if I am honest I have to say that all of those people have that role in my life as individual friends rather than as, if you like, church representatives. It's difficult for me to define since I'm now a church leader myself, but even when I was a member of a church congregation it wasn't often my experience that a whole church managed to really feel like a welcoming community for me as a single person.

This is an area where the church should really be miles ahead of the world around us. We should be getting this right. In the society we live in, the obsession with sex means that people miss out on community, on genuine relationships, in which "family" means more than just the people you're related to. In church we know better than this. We know how to be family.

And that brings me to the good old "family service". I wonder what you think about that one. I'm not generally all that sensitive about which words are used to describe things, but I'm not at all keen on this term. When I first went to the church I now lead they had a "family service" and fairly early on I asked whether it might be possible to change it. I explained that the name made me feel as though it didn't include me, because it made it sound like the people they really wanted there were nice neat little units of mum, dad, and children, and that it was quite possible that anyone who didn't fit into that sort of group would feel left out by it. To be honest I'm not really sure they understood what I was saying. Even some of the other single people didn't feel the same (though some did, so I know it wasn't just me!) Some of them tried to say that by family they meant church family, but I don't think that's what most of them really thought it meant. So after a time we changed the service to be officially called an "all-age service", which I think is a better name in a whole host of ways – although of course there will be some people who never manage to stop calling it a family service!

Alice is in her thirties. She reflects that often churches talk about "family" and, although if pressed they would say that they mean the church community, the word itself can feel excluding to those who are single – for example "family services" may feel like something that single people are not welcome to. In her experience there was lots of teaching on singleness when she was a teenager and then a young adult, but there tends to be less in the normal church teaching programme. She enjoys being able to be "part of the family" with close friends, just joining in with whatever they're doing. This is also helpful as a reminder that marriage and family life aren't always perfect! Having said that, she finds it hard when friends talk incessantly about their children. She says, "I don't know if I am called to be single forever, but I do know that I am called to be single today so I want to live in its fullness."

Another big issue for single women is Mothering Sunday. (Guys – apologies. I wonder, is Father's Day similarly difficult for you, even though it is currently still a largely secular festival?) Going to church on Mothering Sunday can feel like a huge undertaking for single women because of the potential for pain that lies ahead. I know several women who simply stay at home on Mothering Sunday every year. As a church leader that's not an option for me, although of course I can hopefully make sure that our service is positive, inclusive, and helpful!

I'm sure that what all churches set out to do on Mothering Sunday is to celebrate mothering in all its forms. However, in practice what often happens is that some women find the experience painful for a variety of different reasons – obviously it isn't only single women who struggle with it. It can be hard if the whole service feels as if it is only for those who are mums, and some single women find themselves aching because they don't fit into that category and are terrified that they never will. The giving out of flowers, so common in many churches, can be the hardest part of all, as well-meaning adults shove small children towards childless married women and single women, so as not to "leave them out". The irony is that I, and many others I have spoken to, would much rather be left out than artificially included into a category of which we are not really a part (although I do also know many single women who love to receive these flowers).

Of course I'm not saying that we should abandon all Mothering Sunday services – it's great that we celebrate mothering and motherhood. There are lots of possibilities, however, to celebrate Mothering Sunday in ways in which those who don't have children of their own, or those who find it difficult for any number of other reasons, can still enjoy and take part. At my church we don't give out flowers, but the Sunday School make gifts for all the adults, which are then distributed during the service. We celebrate all the great things about the day, we celebrate the great job that mums do, we celebrate "mothering" in all its forms, and we also acknowledge those for whom it is a struggle.[9]

Where do I fit in?

The fourth issue for single people in churches can simply be a feeling of not quite fitting in, and of other people treating them differently, or even not quite knowing what to do with them.

Sometimes it can feel as though we're constantly being questioned about our single status. "So, have you got a boyfriend yet?" enquire friends, old ladies, and random strangers we happen upon in church. Kristin Aune has written a book in which she surveyed many single women on a whole range of topics. The book has some fantastic comebacks for questions such as this. When asked "Are you still single?" it suggests a reply of "Yes, are you still married?" Or, when asked "How's your love life?" a reply of "Fine thanks, how's your sex life?"[10] I often threaten, to my mum's horror, to use this on a friend of hers who assails me with that question every time I see her, but of course we both know that I would never actually have the nerve!

Linked to this can be people's constant efforts to matchmake. There's a danger of the church being seen as a dating agency, with any stray single people who chance to walk through the door being pounced upon or terrified away. The matchmaking thing is fine if you're up for it, and if you've given people permission to do it, but it's patronizing and unhelpful if you haven't! I have friends who have told me of occasions when they have innocently turned up for dinner with friends to find themselves clearly having been set up, and the whole occasion has been horribly awkward and embarrassing for the two poor single people. If you are up for it though, your church can definitely help out with matchmaking. Married people within the church could host events where singles can meet one another and get to know each other in an unpressured way. There are also Christian dating websites, and groups which run social events.

One final thing which I think churches (and particularly church leaders and speakers) could do is to mind their language! It often seems to me that the default position that people speak about in churches is of being married with a few small children. So, when illustrations are given in a talk, or when some sort of generic language is needed, it tends to describe that sort of family unit. The assumption often seems to be that everyone has a spouse, and everyone has children, and everyone's life involves a wedding day, going on honeymoon, doing the school run, making packed lunches, and so on. The problem with this is that it's incredibly excluding for anyone who doesn't fit into that kind of category. Obviously every person has their own life circumstances and not all of them can always be covered – but making an effort to be a bit more inclusive would be really helpful.

Hope is in her thirties and has never been married. She feels that her church sometimes lacks the imagination to understand how simple things can be painful – for example, they often don't realize that arriving at and leaving from social events alone can feel awkward and tiring, especially when you don't know many people there. Someone once commented how "brave" she was to come to an event by herself, which made it far worse – especially as it wasn't backed up with an invitation to join them next time! She has been asked when she's going to get married – as if it were something she could decide upon easily! She tries to take the initiative with hospitality and invite people to her house, but this can be exhausting to do alone, so more recently she has been trying to pay people the compliment of asking them to co-host at her house. She acknowledges that it can be hard to be single at times, and that she might wish things were different, but nonetheless feels that it doesn't define her – "Being single and celibate is not a reason to develop a persecution complex, as if we are the only ones who 'suffer' in the church! We have a responsibility for cooperating with the work of the Holy Spirit in growing us to maturity in Christ, whatever situation we find ourselves in – however difficult or easy we are finding it at the time!"

I really don't want it to sound as though I'm having a go at all of our churches, or at married people in general – that is absolutely not my intention! That's one of the reasons why I wanted to include chapter six in this book, as I think it's really important that we get a dialogue going between married and single people, and that we all make the effort to understand each other a bit more.

I do think, though, that this starts with us all being honest. Very often I have had conversations with single people who are inwardly seething about comments that have been made to them by married people, or about experiences within their churches which have left them feeling deeply hurt and excluded. When such things happen it's easy for us to become angry and bitter and to either shut ourselves off and refuse to engage any more with the people who have hurt us, or to put a lid on the hurt and pretend it isn't there.

I don't think that either of these responses is helpful or healthy. I think that instead we need wherever possible to acknowledge when something has caused us hurt, and raise it in a positive and constructive way. Now obviously this won't always be possible – we're far more likely to be able to have this sort of conversation with someone we know well than we are with a stranger, for instance. It's always better to initiate a conversation when we're feeling calm than when we're angry or upset, and to do so at a time and in a place where there is an opportunity to have a proper discussion. Of course it's highly unlikely that the comment which upset us was meant in a negative way, so hopefully the person will be open to what we have to say. There are times, however, when that won't happen and things will be difficult and awkward – there's always a possibility of that outcome, so really it's a question of weighing things up and deciding whether or not it's worth taking the chance.

I think we do need to take some responsibility here – it's easy to become upset by something that's said, and to allow it to fester away and make us bitter, but that doesn't help anyone. We have a choice whether to raise the issue and have the discussion, or to let it go – and if so, to really move on from it. Whichever choice we make will be better than simply filing it away in a box marked "hurts to be ignored"!

> Julia is in her thirties and is not married. There are people in her church who make an effort to support single people – even organizing a speed dating event. She doesn't like it when some single people fall into the "pity party" mentality. She feels that the wider church should do more to disciple men and to evangelize men. She has noticed that some married friends invite her and other single friends for "casual" dinners but save the "special occasion" dinners for their other married friends. She enjoys looking younger and thinks this is because she doesn't have children! She finds the uncertainty of the future can be difficult – not knowing whether or not her singleness will be for life. She also longs for children and has begun to wonder whether at some point to consider fostering or adopting children by herself.

What about kids?

There is another area that is an issue for lots of single people – although not, of course, all of them. That is the issue of childlessness. (I realize some single people have children, and I apologize if what follows doesn't relate directly to you).

This is a very difficult issue and one which is very emotive but I think, like many of the issues in this area, it is something that is often not talked about enough.

Lots of married couples find themselves sadly unable to have children, for a whole variety of different reasons. I'm not in a position to comment on that personally, although I do have friends for whom it has been a very difficult and painful issue that I have seen them go through. I don't know whether or not childless couples would say that they feel they are well supported by their churches. I hope that they would, but of course I can't know how it feels to be in their situation. I am sure that it must be incredibly difficult to continue to celebrate new pregnancies and new births within the church family when that is the one thing that you long for with all of your heart. I absolutely don't want to minimize or downplay the pain they go through.

However, what I do want to do is discuss the issue of childlessness as it relates to single people. Obviously, if we never marry and if we choose to live celibate lives, then we are not able to have children (unless of course we choose to foster or adopt). And yet I think that the fact that we don't have a spouse is generally considered to be the primary issue, rather than the fact that we don't have children. For many people I speak to, not having children is a huge area of pain. Contrary to stereotypes, I think this is often a big issue for men as well as for women, although of course for women there is a time factor that is more pressing than it is for men – the biological clock that will not stop ticking!

The issues I've mentioned earlier about the attitude of the church towards single people also come into play here. In the same way that "couple" language and events can cause single people to feel alienated, so too can "family" language and events

– as we have seen with the example of Mothering Sunday.

Each single person will choose to deal with this in their own way. I adore children and would dearly love to have my own. Sometimes it's actually painful to spend time around them, because it makes my heart ache for what I don't have. And yet my life is better and richer when I do spend time with children – because they're funny and cute and intelligent and precious! So I choose to surround myself with families and children, and to engage as much as I can with their lives. I love to do children's work at church events because it's a joy and a privilege, and it reminds me of what's really important! I love to have days out with my friends' children and to see their appetite for life and fun. And I love to babysit in order to allow my friends to go out for a bit without their kids – that's something I can do whenever I like, so I choose to bless them in this way.

Some single people might choose not to do these things, because they're just too painful. That's your choice, of course – but make sure you don't try so hard to prevent yourself from being hurt that you also miss out on lots of potential joy.

Being God-obsessed

I've made the case throughout this chapter that the church can, at times, seem as though it is "marriage-obsessed". So how, in the midst of this, do we live a life that is "God-obsessed"? I think that begins to happen when we consciously shift our focus upwards rather than inwards or outwards. Some single people want to get married; others don't. Either way, that's fine, and there's certainly nothing wrong with actively looking for a marriage partner if that's what we want to do. The problem comes when the desire for marriage or children (or, in other contexts, money, or a great job, or new clothes, or reputation, or whatever it is) gets in the way of our desire for God.

If we're not careful, our singleness can actually become the issue – it can so shape and define us that we lose our focus on the really important things. Too many people are obsessed with the wrong things in life – but God is the only healthy obsession there is!

Being God-obsessed is about loving God "with all your heart and with all your soul and with all your strength";[11] it's about putting him first at all times; it's about seeking ways to honour him every day; it's about having "confidence in what we hope for and assurance in what we do not see";[12] it's about seeing other people as God sees them; it's about resisting sin and temptation; it's about living a life of purity.

Church is messy

Church is the imperfect, messy, human institution that Jesus established to be his body here on earth and to share his good news with the world. Sometimes church is a joy and a blessing, a vision of the new heavens and new earth. But sometimes, because it's run by human beings and made up of human beings, it's a disaster! People argue and fall out, mess up and make mistakes, and hurt one another. But, as someone once said, "The world at its worst needs the church at its best."

For us as single people, church can be our closest family and our dearest friends. It can be the community we long to be part of, the people who laugh with us and cry with us, who are there in the significant moments of our lives. Sometimes it might feel as though the church is marriage-obsessed. But we need – all of us – to make sure that we stay God-obsessed. That way we might just begin to be the church Jesus intended all along.

Chapter 3

Purely single

Paul encouraged the Philippians to think about "whatever is pure".[1] It's good advice for all Christians, of course. But for single Christians, what does it mean for us to seek to live a pure life? I'm not talking here just about sex, though that is part of it (and we'll be looking at that more in chapter four). I'm also talking about how our minds, our hearts, our speech, our actions, and our whole life can be kept pure. What will that look like?

Paul reminds the Thessalonians:

As for other matters, brothers and sisters, we instructed you how to live in order to please God, as in fact you are living. Now we ask you and urge you in the Lord Jesus to do this more and more. For you know what instructions we gave you by the authority of the Lord Jesus. It is God's will that you should be sanctified: that you should avoid sexual immorality; that each of you should learn to control your own body in a way that is holy and honourable, not in passionate lust like the pagans do, who do not know God; and that in this matter no one should wrong or take advantage of a brother or sister. The Lord will punish all those who commit such sins, as we told you and warned you before. For God did not call us to be impure, but to live a holy life. Therefore, anyone who rejects this instruction does not reject a human being but God, the very God who gives you his Holy Spirit."[2]

So a pure life is one in which God comes first, in which what he wants is more important than what we want. It's one in which we seek to become more like him, and more like the people he has made us to be. It's one in which we recognize that we are works in progress, that there will always be more of God for us to learn about, discover, and experience.

A pure life is one that is free from jealousy, bitterness, and resentment

It's so easy, isn't it, to fall into feeling jealous of those around us who have what we don't have, what we want, or what we think that we need. In our society jealousy is often positively encouraged. It's jealousy that sells products, because that is what adverts seek to create when they show us a product or a lifestyle that is different from our own, and slowly but surely suck us into believing that everything would be better if only we had that thing for ourselves.

When we see a car that goes so much faster than ours; a woman with hair so much sleeker than ours; a kitchen that is so much more practical than ours – we become jealous. We want that car, that hair, that kitchen. We convince ourselves that our life will be so much better once we have them.

And then because we can't afford them, or because we buy them and they turn out not to actually change our lives after all, we become bitter and resentful. We become angry with anyone who does have those things, anyone whose life seems better, or richer, or easier, or more beautiful than ours. But the fact that society seems to want us to think and to act this way doesn't mean that there is no alternative. We always have a choice. We can make a decision not to be taken in by these things. (One very practical way to help this along is to simply turn off the television when the adverts come on, or at least to mute the volume – that way we can avoid just for a few moments the subtle but insistent whine of our consumer society.)

Let me explain. We cannot always affect or alter the situations around us and the circumstances in which we find ourselves. But we can make a choice about what our response to those circumstances will be. We can choose joy, a fruit of the Spirit, and allow it to grow, bloom, and blossom in our lives.

Joy isn't affected by the particular and specific events that are taking place in our lives at any one time. Joy is a state of mind and heart, a state of being. Joy doesn't come from what is happening in the world around us, but from somewhere deep inside. It isn't affected by the ups and downs of life because it is built on something firmer and stronger than that. It is true, in a strange but ultimately very real and comforting way, to say that as Christians we are able to be joyful when life is hard

79

as well as when it is good, when things are not going well as well as when they are, when we are unhappy as well as when we are happy.

Amy Carmichael put it like this: "Joy is not gush. Joy is not mere jolly-ness. Joy is perfect acquiescence – acceptance, rest – in God's will, whatever comes. And that is so, only for the soul who delights in God."

The joy that we have as Christians is built on the foundation of our faith in God and all that we know about him. We know that he created us. We know that he loves us. We know that he sent Jesus to earth to live among us, and to die in our place, and to rise again so that we might be forgiven. We know that he listens to us when we talk to him. We know that he is interested in every part of our lives. We know that if we give our lives to him and follow him we will one day live with him forever. And so we can be filled with joy no matter what life throws at us and no matter how tough things get.

Jesus doesn't want us to live a life of jealousy, bitterness, and resentment, because those things diminish us and make us less than we can be and should be. A life lived that way is a half life, and Jesus wants us to have a full life. Indeed, he tells us that this is why he came: "The thief comes only to steal and kill and destroy; I have come that they may have life, and have it to the full."[3]

If we truly live a life that is full – full of love, full of joy, full of fun, full of friendships, and most of all full of Jesus – then we won't need to live a life of jealousy, bitterness or resentment; in fact, there will simply be no room for those things to exist.

Luke is in his forties and finds his church neither supportive nor unsupportive, but is happy with that as "singleness is not something I look to my church for support with". He values being part of mixed social gatherings that include both married and single people. Luke chooses to share a house with others and finds that helpful in terms of having company, but also as it prevents him from developing selfish lifestyle habits. He highlights the potentially different issues for men and women who are single, as men may be viewed with more suspicion, for example if they attend social events alone. He values having more flexibility and freedom in how he spends his time and money.

A pure life is one that is free from greed and selfishness

John Stott, the famous minister, preacher, and author, who has now gone to be with the Lord, never married. He said of single people that "Apart from sexual temptation, the greatest danger which I think we face is self-centredness."[4]

As single people (if we don't have children), then we only have ourselves to think about when making decisions, which could lead to selfishness and self-indulgence. Now you might say, "Well, why does that matter? If there's only me to worry about then surely it's up to me what I do, and not anyone else." But the point is that selfishness is simply not a godly characteristic. We are all called to put other people's needs ahead of our own, so that's what we must do. And if we are selfish it will affect all of our other relationships – the truth is that there is never actually just ourselves to think about.

We are all part of a huge network of friendships and relationships. Most of us are part of some sort of family network, a friendship group, a church fellowship, a work environment, and a neighbourhood community. There are people among whom we live and work, and with whom we interact regularly. The decisions that we make in life will inevitably have a bearing on some of them as well, so we can never see ourselves as totally free to do as we wish.

Of course the opposite of self-centeredness can also be true, which is that we focus on other people's needs and neglect our own, and don't look after ourselves properly. Both are to be avoided – we need to find the middle ground. Actually, as single people we do have a huge opportunity in the way we use our time. We have an opportunity to serve others because we may have if not *more* free time, then at least more flexibility in how we use our free time.

We also have a fantastic opportunity as single people for intimacy with God. Obviously that should be a priority for all Christians, but for married people and people with children there are others in their lives who need to be given a huge amount of time and energy. So for us as single people, especially if we don't have children, we may find that we have opportunities to pursue a deep intimacy with Jesus, which is a very precious and valuable thing. And we have an opportunity for solitude – which isn't the same as loneliness. We have the opportunity to be by ourselves, to be alone with God, to pray, to go on retreat. We can choose to turn potential times of loneliness into times of solitude and blessing. I'm not saying it's easy! But we can do it.

> Harriet is in her forties. She feels her singleness isn't an issue in her church – she holds positions of responsibility in various ministries there and hasn't found her singleness to be a barrier. She doesn't like the idea of specific groups for single people: "I actually find this unhelpful as I feel they draw attention to my singleness and what I want is 'family'." She values it when married friends talk about when they were single, rather than never mentioning it, and also when they talk in a balanced way about marriage, rather than pretending that it's always 100 per cent wonderful. She values the freedom that singleness brings to make her own decisions and to develop ministries because of having more flexibility – but recognizes that the flip side of this is the possibility of becoming selfish or self-absorbed, since there's no one on hand to be accountable to.

A pure life is one that is honest and self-aware

I think we need to be realistic and honest with ourselves about which things are more likely to be a problem for us. If you find it hard to walk into events on your own, then make sure you arrange to share cars when you're going to parties, or to church events, or whatever. If you find Sunday afternoons hard after church, then try to arrange walks, or meals, or other activities, with friends for that time. If you find it hard when you get in from work or from meetings, then arrange with a friend that you'll phone them to chat over how it went. If you find holidays hard, look into travel companies that cater for single people, where you can go on your own but be in a group. I've done this for the last few years and have had some fantastic holidays all over the world.

We run the risk of either not being busy enough and falling into lazy patterns of life, or of being too busy, overcommitting ourselves, and not taking the necessary amount of time off for rest and recreation. If we live alone then there is no one around to encourage us to get up and about and do things, or to encourage us to stop and take a break. This relates to all sorts of things to do with how we live. It's important to eat well and have a balanced diet, to get enough sleep, to get enough exercise, to have a well-balanced life in all senses. With no one around to see what we do and how we spend our time, we have to make sure we're disciplined and self-controlled. Again, it's worth putting things in place to help with this. If you struggle to get round to going to the gym, you could arrange to meet a friend there at a regular time each week, and then go for a coffee afterwards. If you struggle to cook and eat well, you could go to cookery classes, or share recipes with friends, or arrange to eat with someone once a week, alternating between your house and theirs. If you know you have a tendency to say yes to everything and to fill your diary, you could get a friend to commit to reminding you to take time off, and perhaps even to agree to show them your diary every week or month so they can check you're doing it.

These things might sound a bit regimented or false, but it's by getting to know ourselves, working out what makes us tick, how we function, and what we need, that we'll be better equipped to live healthy, balanced lives and to avoid the potential temptations and pitfalls. You might also think, "This is all very well, but there's no one I can ask to do this stuff." That might be true in some cases, but I bet it's true for fewer of us than initially think it. If you have got a close friend or family member whom you trust, why not ask them? If you are part of a church small group, ask someone there. If there's someone else at church you feel you could trust, you could ask them.

But it's not enough just to talk about what "they" need to do – we need to take some responsibility for this stuff ourselves. It isn't good enough to get upset when people say things we consider to be hurtful if we never explain to them why that is. It isn't good enough to bemoan the lack of community in our church if we never make any attempt to foster it. It isn't good enough to say how valuable inter-generational friendships are if we never try to make any. Sometimes if we want something like this to happen then we have to put in a bit of work.

Hazel is in her forties and is divorced with children. She has close friends at church who are very supportive and she says that "they are aware of my workload as a single parent and working mum, and never put on me". She does, however, sometimes feel that in her large church she is pressured to sign up to help with things which she doesn't have the time to do because of her family responsibilities. Being single has enabled her to delight in the fact that "God is the lover of my soul". The thing she would say she most misses in being single is having someone to talk to and give their advice from a male viewpoint.

A pure life is one that is countercultural and goes by God's values rather than by the world's

In his letter to the Romans, Paul urges his readers to live differently to the society around them:

> So here's what I want you to do, God helping you:
> Take your everyday, ordinary life—your sleeping,
> eating, going-to-work, and walking-around life—
> and place it before God as an offering. Embracing
> what God does for you is the best thing you can
> do for him. Don't become so well-adjusted to your
> culture that you fit into it without even thinking.
> Instead, fix your attention on God. You'll be
> changed from the inside out. Readily recognize
> what he wants from you, and quickly respond to it.

Unlike the culture around you, always dragging you down to its level of immaturity, God brings the best out of you, develops well-formed maturity in you."[5]

There are so many situations in which Christians are called to live differently from those around them. There's a t-shirt that can be bought at festivals and is popular with Christian young people. It shows a huge number of fish, all identical, and all swimming in the same direction. Then there is one fish that looks different from all the rest and is swimming in the opposite direction. Often this is how it can feel to us – that we are the only one going this way and that we're constantly swimming against the tide.

As Christians, our decisions and our values, and the way we choose to live our lives, are based on the Bible with the mandate it sets out before us, and on the guidance of the Holy Spirit. Sometimes this will mean that the people around us, and perhaps even our closest family and friends, will think that we are crazy. Sometimes it will mean that we will find ourselves being the only one to make a stand on a particular issue. Sometimes it will mean that we face misunderstanding, teasing, or even ridicule because of the choices we make.

God's values and the world's values are often at odds with one another, as the values of God's kingdom are very often markedly different from the values of our society. And when we find ourselves facing a conflict and with a choice to make, the choice must always be to live God's way. The previous passage from Romans is clear – we must not become so well adjusted to the world around us that we fail to question it. Rather, as we choose to live for God, we find ourselves transformed as we become more and more the people he has called us to be.

You might have heard the story about a frog being boiled. The premise is that if you have a saucepan of boiling water and you drop a live frog into it, the frog will immediately squeal and jump out. It knows that a pan of boiling water is not a good place to be and so it gets away as quickly as it can. However, if you put a frog into a saucepan of cold water and then gradually heat it up, the frog will not move. It will stay in the pan until it is boiled alive – because the temperature only changes gradually, the frog doesn't notice what is happening. I have no idea whether or not this is true, and I have no intention of doing an experiment to find out, but whether it is true or not, the lesson we can learn is the same. Sometimes the circumstances around us can change and the situation in which we find ourselves can become harmful. If we're not paying careful attention, we won't notice until it's too late.

It seems to me that sometimes our society can have the same sort of effect on us as the gradually boiling water supposedly has on the frog. We have been part of it for so long, we have unconsciously absorbed its attitudes and values, and so we often fail to notice how damaged much of it is. Of course there are many good, noble, and honourable things in our society, but there are also many that are unwholesome and unhealthy. If Christians from another part of the world suddenly arrived in our culture today, they would realize that much of it is self-centred, and is driven by money, sex, power, and greed. We live in a society which very often condemns more than it forgives; which judges more than it shows mercy; which encourages dishonesty and greed more than honesty and generosity; which hates more than it loves.

As Christians we are called to live in a different way to this. We follow the One who gave up his life so that we might have eternal life. The values of God's kingdom are radically different from the values of our society. Love, grace, mercy, kindness, forgiveness, peace, faithfulness, courage, and justice rule.

As single people, then, these values should affect much of how we live. Our lives ought to be countercultural, and they ought to attract attention from people around us who see that we live differently and wonder why. We can model lives that put Jesus at the centre and put his commands ahead of our needs and desires.

Rebecca is in her thirties. Being single isn't really an issue for her. As she puts it: "I don't think of myself as being single; I clearly am but it's not at the forefront of my identity." She finds her church and her friends to be supportive of her as a person but doesn't feel that this is particularly related to being single. She values the fact that her married friends always make her feel welcome and she never feels as though she's a third wheel when she's with them. She says that it's sometimes difficult to not have one special person who she can call on first, but recognizes that this can also be a positive as it means that she has to lean more on God.

A pure life is one that is free from discontent

It is very easy to give in to feelings of discontent and allow ourselves to be unhappy. You might think that sounds strange – surely being unhappy is something which just happens to us, which cannot be helped? Well, I'm not sure that's true. Obviously some people at some times are affected by depression or other illnesses that can impair their mood and make life feel very dark and difficult. But for those of us not affected in this way, I think we have a bit more of a choice about how we live, and about what our state of mind is.

There can be a danger for always-single people that we become unhappy and bitter because we feel that we've missed out. And yes, it's true – if we never marry and we never have children, then we do miss out on those things, of course we do. There will be a lack in our lives because those things have not happened for us. But what we need to remember is that those things were never ours in the first place. We don't have a "right" to have them. They are wonderful, exciting, enriching things for those people who do have them. But they are not vital to life. And for those of us who don't have them, their lack does not mean that our lives cannot be full and rich.

In missing out on those things there will be numerous other blessings and opportunities that will come our way that wouldn't have done so otherwise. Our lives can still be full, but they will be full of slightly different things, and will work out in slightly different ways. It may be true that the grass always looks greener on the other side of the fence, but all we've got is our grass, the grass we've been given, right here, right now, so let's live with it and make the most of it, and look for the joys it can bring.

I know that I can be tempted to feel discontented in my singleness. For as long as I can remember, I have wanted to get married and have children. I know that's true for a lot of people, though by no means for all. As a little girl I had my wedding day all planned out, and had even picked names for my children! I just assumed that I'd go out with a few boys, and then meet one I loved, who loved me, and we'd get married, and that would be that. As I grew up and the years went by I began to realize that things weren't going to happen quite that smoothly. I vividly remember reaching my sixteenth birthday, and then my eighteenth, and then my twenty-first, and most recently my thirtieth, and every time thinking, "Hmm, still not happened then." I don't know why it is that "milestone" birthdays make it feel more real, but they just do, don't they?

For me, the pain of still being single was compounded by the fact that I've never been out with anyone, so I found myself thinking that I must be unattractive, that no one must ever have fancied me or been interested in me, and so asking what was wrong with me. When people attempted to be kind and enquired about boyfriends, or tried to reassure me that there was still plenty of time, that just made it worse. And those of you who are single will know that people can really say some pretty unfortunate things, can't they?

Oliver is in his thirties and has never been married, although he has been in long-term relationships in the past, before he became a Christian. He would like to get married and have children one day, and would hope to meet someone who shares his faith. In his previous church he found it difficult because most people were older than him and there was no one else in the same stage of life as him. In his current church there are lots of younger people and so he finds it easier to fit in, and easier to find people to talk to and share with. He has friends he can go out with for a drink, but finds it hard if everyone else brings their partner and he feels like a gooseberry.

And so I find myself here, aged thirty-four and single. And at this point I think that there's a choice that needs to be faced. How will we live? I think of this as a choice between being a tortoise and being a sunflower. (Bear with me, I promise to explain!)

The question is this – will you give in to the feelings of discontent and allow yourself to turn into a tortoise, pulling your shell around you for protection? It's tempting, certainly. It might feel like the easier, safer option, and perhaps it is, at least in the short term. When you are protected by your shell, nothing can get near you, so nothing can harm you. You can become bitter and dwell on all the things you don't have, all the things you would like to have, all the things you feel you've missed out on, what you consider to be the unfairness of it all. You can look at friends with envy and jealousy and wish that you had what they have. You can live a half-life, a life of if-onlys and what-ifs. But that is so much less than the full life that Jesus wants for you.

Or you can make a different choice. You can turn your back on feelings of discontent and choose joy instead, the sunflower option. You can turn your face upwards towards the sun – or, more accurately, the Son. A sunflower is a beautiful thing that cannot fail to make you smile when you look at it. It's brightly coloured and fun, and reminds us of warm days and sunshine. A sunflower is also fragile. Choosing this option might not always be the safer option. It might mean, certainly in the short term, that there is actually more pain and difficulty. But over time this will be the best choice by far. It is the choice of vulnerability, of allowing others into your lives and choosing to open yourself up to them.

The choice to become a sunflower rather than a tortoise means that you can focus on the blessings you have in your life; you can seek out the good things that life has to offer; you can grab each challenge that comes your way and embrace it.

I've made a choice that I'm going to live my life as a sunflower rather than as a tortoise. It isn't always easy. Please don't imagine that I'm saying I've got this all sussed and sewn up. That most definitely isn't the case. Sometimes I fail and allow myself to wallow for a while in the tortoise zone. The shell comes up and I disappear inside it and it's a dark place to be. But being a sunflower is a choice I try to make each day. It has to be an active process, a day-by-day grace that I ask God for in order to keep going. These sorts of decisions aren't ones we make once and then tick the box and say, "That's that sorted, then." These are decisions that need to be remade and reaffirmed every day. But if that's the case then that's what we must do. I don't want to be bitter and unhappy. I don't want to be jealous and resentful. I don't want to live in discontent. I don't want to waste time thinking about the things I haven't got. I want to be thankful for all the good things that I do have and spend time enjoying them.

I have a job that I love and am passionate about. I live in a gorgeous house with a stunning view. I own a car. I have enough money to live on and to be generous with. I have the freedom to make my own decisions. I am blessed with lots of wonderful friendships. I have three gorgeous godchildren who bring light and love and laughter to my life, and give fabulous cuddles! I travel, go to the cinema and the theatre, eat out, go on great holidays. I refuse to put my life on hold because of what may or may not happen in the future, and because I'm discontented with what I feel I've been dealt as my lot in life.

Paul, in his letter to the church at Philippi, wrote these words:

> Actually, I don't have a sense of needing anything personally. I've learned by now to be quite content whatever my circumstances. I'm just as happy with little as with much, with much as with little. I've found the recipe for being happy whether full or hungry, hands full or hands empty. Whatever I have, wherever I am, I can make it through anything in the One who makes me who I am.[6]

94

For me, the sunflower choice is to be "just as happy" being single. I've learnt (no, let's be realistic, *I'm learning* – and will go on learning, I hope, until the day I go to be with Jesus) to be content whatever my circumstances. And this contentment isn't a nice, easy, floaty, flowery feeling that surrounds me. No, it's a decision that I very deliberately make every day, through gritted teeth and with clenched hands if necessary. But that is my choice. I choose a full life – what do you choose?

Chapter 4

Living a God-obsessed life in a sex-obsessed world

Let us think for a moment about the culture in which we live. It often feels to me as though our society is obsessed with sex. I don't want to be overly critical of the world around us, or to say it's all terrible and evil and we should shun it. It is God's world and of course there are many beautiful, good, and admirable things within it. But it is nevertheless true that the world is not as it should be, and that good is not the only force at work within it. Sadly, the culture of the world, particularly in our postmodern Western society, has become one in which, relationally and sexually speaking, anything goes. And so to live within this world is to be constantly bombarded with images, messages, pictures, headlines, and ideas which reinforce that, and which it is easy to be influenced by and drawn into.

There are just so many sexual messages and images all around us. On television we see advert after advert using sex to sell a product that has nothing at all to do with sex. I'm sure you can recall, even from just the past few years, adverts

97

for chocolate, fizzy drinks, shampoo and cars that shamelessly (and needlessly) used sexual imagery. These adverts are not restricted to late at night either – they are shown throughout the day on mainstream channels when children will be watching. It's not just adverts though – almost every soap opera, drama, and film portrays sex outside marriage as something which is totally acceptable and which everyone is doing.

And it's not just on the television – we're confronted with these images all around us on billboards too, as half-naked people or cavorting couples are used to sell any product. And many magazines have pictures or words on the front cover which can be distracting and unhelpful to us as we pass by, and which are totally unsuitable for children to be exposed to.

Well, at the risk of sounding like a twenty-first century Mary Whitehouse, I think that our culture is obsessed with sex!

I wonder whether it shocks us that we are exposed to these images everywhere we turn, or if it just seems normal to us because it's what we are used to seeing. It seems that we, as a nation, are saying that we are happy not just for ourselves but also for our children to be presented with such images. But these pictures and concepts are not harmless. We need to be incredibly careful about what we watch and read – images and ideas can become planted into our minds and begin to rot away all that is right and pure.

What we are being told over and over again by all of these images, implicitly and explicitly, is that sex sells; that it is a commodity and a right; that if you're not having it you're not normal; and that the sooner and the more often you have it the better a person you will be.

We are also told "spiritual lies" – the devil plants the idea in our mind that we cannot live without sex. This is not true, and we can choose to declare this. We can be fulfilled without sex – it isn't necessary to our happiness. In contrast, though, the prevailing cultural world view is that sex is necessary not just to our happiness, but to our very survival.

This kind of attitude seems to prevail in every sphere of life. I wonder if you have ever had the sort of conversation where it suddenly becomes clear that the person speaking to you is beginning to think that you are some sort of oddity because your usual Friday night pastime is not going out to bars or clubs, drinking ten vodkas, and sleeping with someone whose name you don't know. Now I know that I'm caricaturing there and perhaps unfairly critiquing parts of our culture, but there have often been times when I, as a young(ish!) single woman, have felt that pressure.

I vividly remember a conversation over lunch when I was at university, between myself, another Christian friend who had recently got engaged, and some of our non-Christian course mates. They understood that as Christians we believed that sex should be only between marriage partners, but it was almost funny to watch the penny drop as the implications of what that meant began to dawn on them. They were teasing my friend about her wedding night and she was taking it in good part, even as they expressed astonishment that she could have made it to twenty-one as a virgin. Then they turned to me and said, "So, you're a virgin too?" Yes, I agreed that I was. "So, you're going to wait until you're married to have sex too?" Yes, again I agreed that was true. "So, if you never get married… wow!" I actually wanted to laugh as the horror of following that train of thought showed on their faces.

But of course it isn't always funny. It isn't always good-natured teasing – sometimes instead it's outright mocking. The pressure doesn't always come from outside, but can also come from within us as we wrestle with our own desires and temptations.

So our world is a world that is, I believe, sex-obsessed. It's a world in which not only are we often mocked for choosing to live chaste lives, but one in which we are actually sometimes not believed. I remember a battle I had with a GP who was trying to persuade me to have a smear test, and I was trying to ask him whether I really needed one, given that I was a virgin. It was very clear from his attitude that he simply didn't believe me. I wondered why on earth he thought that I would lie about it. The reaction to my saying I'd slept with 100 men would presumably have been that that was fine, it was my choice; but the reaction to my saying that I had never slept with anyone appeared to be "You're either lying or there's something wrong with you."

For us as Christians, though, there's a different way to live. Paul writes to the Romans, urging them: "Do not conform to the pattern of this world, but be transformed by the renewing of your mind. Then you will be able to test and approve what God's will is – his good, pleasing and perfect will."[1]

What will it look like for us to not conform, but to test and approve God's will? The best place to begin as we explore that is with God's word.

The Bible says very clearly that sex is a good thing, that it is a gift from God, that it is for enjoyment and for the procreation of children. However the Bible also says very clearly that sex is a gift that is given for married people only.

The only place for sexual activity is within a committed marriage relationship between a man and a woman. Therefore, if we are not married, we shouldn't be having sex, and if we are married, we should only be having sex with the person we are married to. Right at the beginning of the Bible, in the book of Genesis, we read that "God created mankind in his own image, in the image of God he created them; male and female he created them. God blessed them and said to them, 'Be fruitful and increase in number; fill the earth and subdue it.'"[2]

Now I don't know what you're thinking as you read that. It could be, "Well of course, I agree, that is obviously what the Bible says." It could be, "Well that's all very well for you to say, but it's really hard." It could be, "Oh, don't be ridiculous, no one really believes that any more." Or it could be, "I know that's true but I've fallen, I've got it wrong, I've messed up and I don't know what to do." So let's think about this a bit more.

The Bible tells us that sex is only for within marriage

Later on in Genesis, God establishes marriage as his norm for men and women in relationship together:

> But for Adam no suitable helper was found. So the
> Lord God caused the man to fall into a deep sleep;
> and while he was sleeping, he took one of the man's
> ribs and then closed up the place with flesh. Then
> the Lord God made a woman from the rib he had
> taken out of the man, and he brought her to the
> man. The man said, "This is now bone of my bones
> and flesh of my flesh; she shall be called 'woman'
> for she was taken out of man." That is why a man
> leaves his father and mother and is united to his
> wife, and they become one flesh.[3]

This is the context in which family life is established at the outset. Adam and Eve are created, they become one flesh, and they have children.

So God's ideal for us is that if we marry, then we have sex within that marriage, which is enjoyable and may have the potential to bring forth children. If we're not married then the possibility of having sex is simply not an option that is available to us. I believe this is true whether we are straight or gay, and I believe that Christian marriage is a state that can only exist between a man and a woman. Therefore, if we are unmarried, God's ideal for us is to be celibate.

It is clearly true, therefore, that sex outside of marriage (that is, adultery) is unacceptable. When marriage vows are made they are holy and binding, and engaging in sex outside of a marriage goes against God's will and plan.

It is also clearly true that sex before marriage is unacceptable. People sometimes try to justify sex before marriage, especially in a context where a loving couple are faithful to one another and are sure that they will get married one day, perhaps even quite soon. However, sex is something which should be saved for within marriage. What a gift it is to be able to approach our wedding day knowing that we have saved ourselves for that person and that moment. Something deeply profound and mysterious takes place when two people have sex. It is not simply an animal act of passion and pleasure as the world would have us believe. It is so much more than that. It is the becoming "one flesh" that Genesis speaks of and it is far too important to enter into casually.

It's worth saying that I consider these biblical mandates to be for Christians rather than those who are not yet Christians. This is the way in which we choose to live life once we have got to know the Lord of life. Before people know him they have no reason for living life this way. The rules of the kingdom only make sense once you get to know the King! Having said that, I do nevertheless believe that these kingdom rules are the best way for all people to live. They are the Maker's instructions – and he knows what is best for us.

With all of these statements that I'm making about sex I want to be really clear that although I believe this is God's ideal plan, I am absolutely certain that if you have stepped outside of that plan, or even turned your back completely on it and headed in the other direction, it is never too late for you to come back. For all sorts of reasons, you may have not lived your life up to this point in accordance with this plan.

Whenever I have spoken on this topic I have had people come up to me at the end of the session who have wanted to talk to me, and basically what they have needed to do is to confess some previous sexual sin. Maybe when they were very young they lost their virginity and now, years later and single, they feel guilty and wonder whether they are being punished. Maybe before they became a Christian they lived a promiscuous lifestyle and they dare not tell any of their Christian friends for fear of being judged. Maybe they had a period of time when they turned away from their faith and acted in ways which they now regret. Maybe while in a serious and committed relationship with a Christian partner, which they were sure would lead to marriage, they went "too far" – but then the relationship broke up and the reality hit them that virginity isn't something you can get back once it's gone.

So if you have engaged in sex before or outside of marriage, there is forgiveness and a new start available to you through Jesus. In him there is no condemnation. It is, however, necessary to fully repent of any previous lifestyle that wasn't honouring to God. God forgives anyone who comes to him with genuine repentance – but repentance is about more than just saying sorry. Repentance is about turning around, turning our backs on the sin and turning towards God, whose arms are always open.

The Bible tells us that Christians should only marry other Christians

This is hard, because it makes the pool within which we must look for a partner so much smaller. But I do believe that it's the right thing to do. Paul, writing to the Corinthians, warns us:

> Do not be yoked together with unbelievers. For
> what do righteousness and wickedness have in
> common? Or what fellowship can light have
> with darkness? What harmony is there between
> Christ and Belial? Or what does a believer have in
> common with an unbeliever?[4]

People may argue that their unbelieving spouse is very accepting of their faith, and very supportive of their involvement with church, and clearly that is often the case. But most people I know who are married to non-Christians would say that there are times when it's very difficult – when they find their value systems and decision-making processes are entirely at odds with one another, or when they feel pressure coming on one side from their spouse and on the other side from their church, and that they feel torn between the two. I know for myself that even within friendships, there is a different quality to those that are with Christians. I have many deep and loving friendships with people who aren't Christians and I thank God for them. But there can be times of misunderstanding and conflict, and things which we are unable to share and which are hard for them to understand, since our whole world view is so totally different. Since our faith is and should be the very centre of our lives and who we are, it's incredibly difficult if the person with whom we share our life doesn't share our faith. Marriage is difficult enough without going into it with the added complication of a conflict over our faith and beliefs, and different priorities over how we spend our time and money. In addition to this, of course, are the huge positives and benefits that come when both partners share their faith, and can help one another to grow and mature in that faith.

Clearly if you have married a non-believer, or if you have become a Christian since your marriage, this doesn't mean that your marriage is a sham, or that you should separate, or that God isn't interested in your relationship. God believes very strongly in marriage and he wants all marriages to be successful. And within your marriage to a non-Christian you have an amazing opportunity to witness to faith in Jesus. But I would suggest that if you are currently single and looking for a marriage partner, then that person should be someone who shares your faith.

Beth is in her thirties and would like to marry, but would only ever want to marry someone who shares her faith, saying "I think relationships are a challenge enough without taking God out of it." She feels her church is supportive of her because it functions as a family, and so all "family members" are supported, and all activities are open and inclusive. She struggles with not having anyone to share the big experiences of life with.

I also believe that masturbation is not a helpful or healthy practice for us as Christians

I don't see anywhere in Scripture where it is explicitly forbidden, and I have heard some people argue that since it isn't actually "sex with someone you're not married to", then it's OK. But I believe, and I do write as someone who has personally wrestled with this issue and who has spoken to a number of people for whom it has been an issue, that it can become a very unhealthy thing associated with fantasies and obsessions, which can lead to an awful lot of guilt and shame. There's a view that masturbation helps to satisfy sexual desires and release sexual tension, but I don't think this is true. Rather, I think it often intensifies and increases those desires. I think it's far better to avoid masturbating altogether if you can, and to avoid being drawn into this cycle.

If you are someone for whom this has been or is currently an issue, again, there is – as always – love and forgiveness in Jesus. If the word sex is a taboo in most churches, then surely masturbation must be one of the most unlikely words to ever hear uttered inside a church building! But I think this is all wrong. Don't worry, I'm not suggesting it should be something we chat about every week over coffee. But if Jesus came to bring us life in all its fullness, if Jesus is interested in every part of our lives, if Jesus was tempted in every way as we are and yet was without sin, and if Jesus wants us to become more like him – then there should be nothing that we're afraid to speak out loud. Sin, evil, guilt, and shame thrive in the darkness, but when they're brought out into the light they cannot survive.

When we find a safe place to speak about these things, such as a church small group or with a supportive friend or prayer partner, then all of the fear and guilt contained within them disappears, and their power is gone. We *must* be able to speak about these issues in our churches if we're going to really be able to meet people where they are and answer the questions that they are asking.

A temple of the Holy Spirit

This is how Paul refers to our bodies when he writes his first letter to the Corinthians. He reminds them that a sexual sin is a sin against our very body:

> Do you not know that your bodies are temples of the Holy Spirit, who is in you, whom you have received from God? You are not your own; you were bought at a price. Therefore honour God with your bodies.[5]

If our bodies are truly temples in which the Holy Spirit dwells, then it really matters what we do with them. If God himself lives inside of us, then when we sin with our bodies we are sinning against him in a very real, almost physical way. We must treat our bodies (and those of other people) with respect and reverence.

A very practical comment needs to be made here as we think about our bodies. It's very easy for us to be turned on as we look at one another's bodies, so we need to be aware of how we use our bodies. It's perhaps especially true for men that they are very visually aroused, and so us women have to be careful of what we wear, and dress modestly. (Don't worry, that doesn't mean we can't look fabulous!)

We also need to be aware of our behaviour and of the impression that we can give when we act in certain ways. And we need to make sure that we don't put ourselves into situations where it's too easy to mess things up. For instance, if we're single and looking for someone to date, that's great, but let's be careful where we meet them on dates, what we wear, and what we talk about.

Nathan is in his thirties and has never been married. His church is a "welcoming and balanced church that does something for everyone". He would like to get married one day, but being single isn't a problem for him in the meantime. He values time spent with married friends away from their spouse. He enjoys the independence of being single, but misses not having someone around to always rely on.

What does the church have to say?

In Kristin Aune's book,[6] most of the women who were surveyed said that the church doesn't speak or teach enough about sex. They felt the most they were told was "don't have sex outside marriage" and that was it. There was no advice given as to how to cope with this as a long-term lifestyle. They also felt that women and men were treated very differently and stereotypically when it came to the issue of sexual ethics and temptations.

I don't know about you, but I would really agree with that. Very rarely have I heard people in church speaking as part of their regular teaching programme on issues of sex and relationships. And when I have heard people speak on this issue, it has tended to fall along certain lines. When I have heard any teaching on sex it has been addressed solely to married people. Generally, teaching on celibacy and relationships tends to be done for youth groups, as though this is an issue for teenagers, but then when you grow up you will get married so it will be OK and it won't need to be spoken about again. It seems to me, though, that this is just ducking the issue and it isn't good enough.

A few years ago I did a seminar at the New Wine summer conference using much of the material found in this chapter. At the end a group of teenage girls came up to me wanting to chat. They had listened to all that I had said and they had plenty of questions. They were Christian girls, involved in their local church, where they were all part of a youth group. They had all been in relationships, usually, although not always, with Christian boys. They wanted answers. They asked me things like, how far can we go with our boyfriends? What do we say if they want to pressure us to go too far? How do we know when to stop? We chatted for a while and I was as honest as I could be (while reminding them that as someone who has never had a boyfriend I may not have been the best person to ask!). Do you know what they said as they walked away? They thanked me for being so open and honest, and for using "real words" to talk about sex. They said that they had tried to ask their youth workers and church leaders, but that no one would talk to them about this stuff. That made me so sad. These young girls were desperately trying to live pure lives, but no one was helping them to do it. I pray that they found the support they were looking for, that they haven't compromised, and that they are still living God's way.

Often when people do speak about this issue, they tend to imply that for men, the issues involved are to do with pornography and masturbation; and that for women the issues involved are to do with emotional attachment and fantasies. I think this is a huge stereotype. Like all stereotypes, it no doubt has a basis in fact, but I think that we really need to be careful. If this is what we think and say, then it makes life even harder for those men and women who don't fall into the stereotype given for their gender, and so they feel even more excluded and outcast. Most of the women in the Kristin Aune survey said that, contrary to the prevailing view they hear taught in the church, sexual desire was a big issue for them.

So I wonder, do you agree with this analysis that the church doesn't speak enough about the issues of sex and singleness? If you regularly attend church, I wonder if you have heard a sermon on this subject. And if the answer is no, would you like to hear one? What would you like churches to be teaching in this area? What difference would it make to your journey as a single person if these issues were spoken about and taught about more widely? And I wonder too, how many of you feel that the leadership of your church is sensitive to, and supportive of, you as a single person? Maybe you could lend them this book, and begin a conversation with them about how your church could better tackle these issues, and better support single people.

A man called Philip Wilson, a church leader in Ireland, wrote a column in the *Church of England Newspaper* a few years ago entitled "Sex and the Single Christian". He wrote this: "The problem with the church and sex is that it tends to ignore the subject completely or to become obsessed about it in a totally abstract sort of a way."[7] He also talks about the danger of the church teaching only "don't have sex unless you're married", with no support or help given beyond that. He tells a story of a twenty-one-year-old evangelical Christian man he spoke to, who said that he sleeps with his girlfriend. This man said that lots of his friends get married simply so that they can have sex, even though many of them acknowledge that emotionally they do not feel ready for marriage. His reaction to that was to say that marriage was too important to enter into lightly, but that he had sexual desires, so it was better to simply have sex than to enter too early into marriage. But how have we found ourselves at the point where those are the two options that we have been reduced to? The choice shouldn't be between getting married before we're ready and having sex outside of marriage. Neither of these options is healthy nor helpful. Today in the UK, less than 1 per cent of people are virgins when they marry. If, as Christians, we truly believe that this is the best way, the way God wants for us, then we need to change the way we speak and teach about this.

How, then, shall we live?

And what of those for whom at least the choice to enter too early into marriage would be a welcome one? What of those who have always been single, and of those who remain that way throughout their whole lives? What of their sexual desires, their struggle to live a pure life? What should we aspire to in this area, and how do we attain it?

A few years ago there was a fascinating pair of articles about sex and single people in *Third Way* magazine. In one edition there was an article entitled "An Unchosen Chastity" by a woman in her forties who was finding it an almost impossible struggle to live a celibate life.[8] She wrote "Yes, last summer I reached my 40th birthday – and, reluctantly, I'm still a virgin." She argued in passionate and often angry terms that the church needs to rethink its position on sex outside of marriage. She talked of friends who have left the church, unable to cope with the constraints they felt it placed upon them to live up to this ideal. She argued that the Bible forbids sex "outside" marriage (adultery), but not sex "before" marriage, where an unattached and loving couple choose to sleep together. She said that living without sex is easy in one's teens and twenties, but gets progressively harder through the thirties, forties, and beyond. She quoted an older Christian woman who told her, "You should have had an affair in your twenties and repented of it – then at least you'd have the memories." She spoke of numerous friends who have reached a point in their lives when they have decided to begin a relationship with a non-Christian man rather than remain single. She said she feels that the church is embarrassed and confused about its teaching, and says that "I have yet to find anyone with the guts and honesty to admit that 'of course, if you don't find a spouse we expect you to die a virgin', though that is the flipside of the 'no sex before marriage' mantra."

Then, in the next edition of *Third Way* magazine there was an article written from an opposing viewpoint, entitled "A Wild Constraint".[9] The author of this article differs from the first in that she is not a virgin; rather she has had a past filled with various sexual encounters and she spoke of the pain and regrets those have brought. She described the relief of becoming a Christian, which provided her with the capacity and strength to say "no". She paraphrased Paul's teaching in 1 Corinthians about the body being a temple of the Holy Spirit, and said this, "The truth is my body is not my own, just as my country and my life are not my own. It is held in trust for others, for whatever reason God may decide and, as I get older, it's easier to see the value in that."

So where do these two opposing viewpoints leave us? What really is the way in which God wishes us to live as single people? And once we have worked out what the ideal is, how on earth do we actually live it, day after day after day?

Well, while I have huge compassion for the writer of the first article, and do empathize with some of what she says, I nevertheless disagree with her conclusions. She says that she has never found anyone with the guts to say that if we remain unmarried we should die as virgins – well, I have the guts to say that! That is what I believe. That is the path that I have chosen for myself since I believe it's the way God calls me, and all single Christians, to live. I don't know whether or not I will get married, but I do know that if I don't, I will live my whole life as a virgin.

Now please don't think I'm saying that if you have not chosen that path or if you have failed to live up to it then you're living outside of God's will and blessings. That is not at all what I am saying. If you have in the past had sex when you weren't married, but now wish to choose to live a celibate life, that's great. What I am saying is that we need to make a choice about how we live, and to weigh very carefully what God's will is, what the effects of our actions are on us and other people, and how we need to guard our hearts and minds.

Penny is in her thirties. She was engaged in her twenties but the relationship broke down. She says that "getting married and having a family is something I desire above all". There are few single people in her church and she finds that although there is an effort to make events "inclusive", often they have a "family feel" which can lead to her feeling excluded. She has found that teaching on relationships for adult singles can be quite patronizing (and is often done by married couples!). She loves the freedom and independence that come from being single, and has also enjoyed developing some of the practical life skills that she's needed and is now "a dab hand with a hammer!" However she finds loneliness can be a big issue, and as someone who values physical touch, she struggles with a lack of hugs. She says, "I'd much rather find myself as I am now – single – than trapped in a marriage that was wrong simply because I was desperate to fill a void and not be alone."

But seriously, how do we actually *do* it?

So if you are still with me, and if we can agree that this is the ideal way to live as single Christians, that's all very well and good, but how on earth do we actually do it? We have already looked at how obsessed our society is with sex. So how do we live in a way that is radical and countercultural and yet can be genuinely sustained as a way of life day by day?

Well I think there are a few really practical things which can help us with this.

The first point may sound obvious, but I think it's really important that we know who we are and how we are made, so I think we need to really honestly examine ourselves. Our personality and character will have a big effect on the things that become dangers, issues, and temptations for us. The things which for me are triggers will not be the same for you, so there's no point me just telling you what I do. You do need to work this out for yourself, and it is really worth spending some time doing this.

I would encourage you to think about whether you are an introvert or an extrovert. You may have done personality tests such as Myers-Briggs which will have told you this, or you may not be sure which you are. The easiest way I have heard to work out which you are is to ask yourself, after a busy, stressful day at work, how would you prefer to relax and recharge? If the answer is on your own, quietly, at home, then you are probably an introvert. If the answer is meeting up with friends to chat or going to a party, then you are probably an extrovert. Now obviously that is a bit crude and simplistic, and you might be thinking well, sometimes I'm one and sometimes I'm the other, but I think broadly speaking it helps. And I think it helps because we need that sort of relaxation in our lives.

I'm an extrovert and so if I have a day or two off where I haven't planned anything and I don't go out or see anyone, I start to get a bit miserable, and I know from experience that this is not a good way for me to be. So I need to plan in a trip to see a friend, or at least a phone call. If you're an introvert and you have got a very busy week involving lots of people, you may need to plan in some "me" time so you can recharge. This is important because if we don't get to relax in a way that works for us we will just get more and more wound up and tense. I know for me, when I feel like that, I am far more susceptible to the whispers of the devil, and to doing something which I will later regret.

Another really useful tool for getting to know ourselves is the book *The Five Love Languages* by Gary Chapman. It's incredibly simple, and yet I know when I first read it that I realized just how much it makes sense. The idea is that there are five basic ways in which we can receive love. These are words of affirmation, gifts, acts of service, quality time, and physical touch. Chapman says that each of us has one "love language" that is our primary and preferred way of receiving love and that if we don't get enough of that one, we won't feel loved, even if we are receiving all the others. There is a version of the book specifically for single people, relating each gift to living a single life.[10] It's really helpful for working out how to ensure we get a balance between each of the languages, and especially that we receive enough of our primary language. And again, this is so important.

Imagine, for instance, that your primary language is touch, and you are single and live alone, and can go several days at a time without touching another person. That could leave you very susceptible to temptation if someone shows a physical interest in you. Knowing this about ourselves helps us to walk towards right things and away from wrong things. We also need to be careful that we don't fall into other sin at this point – for instance, we may manage to resist sexual sin but in so doing we become bitter and angry and hard-hearted. This is still sin! We need to try our best to turn away from all types of sin.

Another thing that we need to do is to be genuinely honest with ourselves about what our danger points are. When are we most likely to be tempted to sin in this area? What is most likely to turn us on and potentially to lead us into unhelpful behaviours or thoughts? This will be different for everyone. I said earlier that there can be unhelpful stereotypes about men and women. Whichever we are, we just need to be really honest with ourselves and to guard our hearts and minds. I know that I need to be careful about what I watch on TV, and that if something is beginning to be unhelpful I need to turn it off. I need to be even more careful about this late at night, or when I'm away from home. I need to avoid daydreams and fantasies that fill my mind with unhelpful things. It isn't good enough to just shrug our shoulders and say "Oh, our world is full of sexual images, isn't it terrible." We have a choice. We can turn off the TV, close the internet pop-up, not buy the magazine, not read the book, not watch the film, stop the conversation.

Paul reminds us of the need to "take captive every thought". Our thoughts are not our masters; rather we have the power to allow them space or to banish them as is appropriate. If our thoughts are unhelpful then we can take them captive and make them "obedient to Christ."[11] This isn't always easy, but, as always, we have a choice. As soon as an unhelpful thought appears in our mind, we can banish it and replace it with something else.

I often think of something I heard many years ago. I can't remember who it was that I first heard say it, but they said whenever we sit down to watch a film or TV programme or read a book, or before we go somewhere or say something, we should think, "Would I still do this if Jesus were standing here next to me?" And if the answer is no, well... let's rethink what we're doing.

I think there's always a moment in which we have a choice, and we make a decision. It might be a split second moment, but it's there, and very often we're aware of it. It's as if we're standing at a crossroads and there are two paths in front of us – one is the way of temptation and will lead us to sin and danger; the other is the way of holiness and will lead us closer to God. There is *always* the opportunity to make the right choice.

We need to make sure that if we make a choice to not fill our mind with something unhelpful, that we instead fill it with something helpful. You know the joke about being told not to think about elephants? What can you then not get out of your head? If you just sit there and go "I mustn't think about that, I mustn't think about that", well, that's just not going to work. Instead, why not pick up your Bible. My favourite passage when I am struggling with this area is from Philippians: "Whatever is true, whatever is noble, whatever is right, whatever is pure, whatever is lovely, whatever is admirable – if anything is excellent or praiseworthy – think about such things."[12] If what I'm currently thinking of isn't those things, then I try to replace it with something that is. Put on some worship music. Have a favourite book you can read or DVD you can watch which you know you love and which edifies you. Phone a friend, go for a walk, mow the lawn, clean the house – it doesn't matter what it is, just have some strategy available that will distract you from the unhelpful thoughts and instead fill your mind with those that are pure.

I once said this in a seminar I was teaching, and someone laughed a hollow laugh and asked whether I was living on this planet in suggesting that mowing the lawn would somehow miraculously remove the sexual desire that may be filling your mind and body. I am not stupid – I realize this is anything but easy. I'm not talking here about anything that I haven't had to face myself. But we do not need to give in to the desires and temptations that assail us – we can stand against them.

It's a bit like fasting. Fasting is a great spiritual discipline and I try to do it on a regular basis. When I am fasting, when I first get up I feel a bit hungry, but after a cup of tea I'm usually fine for a while, and I actually tend to make it through the morning and into the early afternoon fairly easily. But by late afternoon I'm generally feeling ravenous. Now this is where things can go one of two ways. If I allow myself to dwell on being hungry, to think about all the things that I would like to be eating at that moment, to go into the kitchen and examine the contents of the fridge, and to begin to plan what I will eat the next day, then I am going to find it very hard to continue with the fast. Similarly, I know that it is not a good idea to go to the supermarket when I'm fasting. But if when I begin to feel hungry I occupy myself in some other way then pretty soon I have forgotten that I'm hungry and I can carry on quite happily throughout the rest of the day.

In many ways the issue of sexual desire in our minds is similar. We have the choice as to whether we indulge those thoughts and fantasies, and allow them to remain in our minds, or whether we send them packing and replace them with something else. Martin Luther once said that we can't stop birds from flying overhead, but we can stop them from nesting in our hair![13]

Another thing that I think is really important is to have someone with whom you can share these issues. I don't mean your whole church, or even necessarily your whole small group. This is personal stuff and it doesn't need to be shared with twenty-three people! But it does need to be shared with someone. If this area is an issue for you, talk to someone. Tell them what you struggle with and how you're going to try to work through it, and ask them to keep you accountable, to check up on how you're doing. Perhaps arrange that you will ring them if you're struggling so that you can chat about it, or that they will text you at certain times to see how you're doing. People always feel like this is an impossible thing to do, and I can understand that; it certainly is hard. But sex is not any more of a taboo or any worse a sin than the other things we wrestle with in our Christian lives – or at least it shouldn't be. We would share with a prayer partner a struggle over wanting to speak more about our faith to our non-Christian friends, or wanting to deal with our anger, or wanting to recharge our prayer life – so why not speak about this?

It is also vital that we have healthy and appropriate relationships with the opposite sex, whether they are married or unmarried. This is so important, but it can be a difficult area. Some people say that if you are single you shouldn't ever be alone with a married person of the opposite sex, and shouldn't go to the pub with them or whatever. I would find that hard, and I don't think it's particularly helpful. Some of my very good friends are married Christian men whom I view as brothers, and I don't fancy them in the slightest! There's no chance at all of any sexual temptation occurring, they're just very good mates. And why are we more likely to be tempted to sin with a married friend than a single one? I think if we get too hung up about this stuff then we are in danger of just conforming to what the world says and making sex the most important issue, when it shouldn't be.

But again we need to be honest with ourselves, and to be sensible. If you know you have feelings for one of your married friends, well then obviously don't spend time with them alone. Be aware of yourself, and if ever you sense feelings developing with one of your married friends, take action at once. Don't ever stay overnight with a married friend of the opposite sex if their spouse isn't there. As a single guy and girl, don't stay overnight together by yourselves. Don't get into conversations with them that aren't going to end up in a helpful place. But let's not let worries and fears about sex get in the way of normal, healthy friendships, or we'll just be conforming to what the world has been trying to tell us all along: that there is no such thing as a healthy, loving relationship between a man and a woman that has absolutely nothing to do with sex. As Christians we need to show the world a different way; a way of healthy, wholesome, loving relationship between men and women who love each other as brothers and sisters.

You see, this mustn't just be about the things that we can't do, the things that are forbidden for us, the ways in which we shouldn't live. This isn't only a negative issue. We have thought earlier about some of the positives of being single, and we need to remember that far from simply being a list of "don'ts", the Christian ideal of chastity can be an incredibly freeing, life-enhancing way to live.

Mark is in his forties and has never been married. He values having married friends who look out for him when he needs a friend, who invite him round to spend time with him, and who pray for him. He finds the biggest issue with being single is the loneliness, and describes feeling lonely "even in a room full of people" because there is no one there who is looking out for him.

All you need is grace

An article in the *Church of England Newspaper* written by a single man called Thomas Garvey sums up well what I have been trying to say: "for large numbers of us… chastity is more than a one-off decision to save ourselves for our (possible) wedding nights; it's a day-to-day grace that we pray for to sustain us."[14]

So that's it, at the end of the day. It's the grace that we ask for, and which God will provide, which enables us to navigate the desires, dangers, and temptations that are all around us and to remain pure and chaste before God.

And I honestly believe that the only way to do this, just like the only way to overcome any issue in our life, and indeed the only way to live, is to keep our eyes fixed on Jesus, and to seek him always. As we walk towards Jesus, we'll find that we're walking away from everything else that would get in our way.

Chapter 5

Single again

Everyone is single at some period in their lives. Some never get married and remain single for the whole of their lives. Some get married and that's the end of their experience of singleness. But some get married and then, either because of divorce or the death of their spouse, find themselves single again. This second period of singleness will have some features in common with the first, but it may also look and feel very different.

The whole issue of finding yourself single again is something that brings with it many of its own issues and challenges. As my own experience is of never having been married, I spoke to a number of friends who are divorced or widowed in order to get some of their views and perspectives on how it feels to become single again. You can read some of their thoughts and experiences throughout this chapter.

There are obviously a whole variety of different circumstances around why a marriage might come to an end, and therefore if you find yourself single again you may find yourself feeling devastated, bereaved, relieved, freed, bereft, or any combination of all of these – and other – emotions.

It may be that you have chosen to end the marriage yourself, or at least have been a willing partner in the decision. Of course that doesn't mean that the situation is without an enormous amount of pain and regret, but at least you may have felt an element of free will and involvement in the decisions that have been made. It may be, however, that the decision was not yours, and your spouse left very much against your wishes, leaving you feeling confused and abandoned, especially if the end of the marriage came as a great shock to you. There may also be feelings of shame and guilt, and you may feel that you have failed in some way because your marriage has broken down. Or it may be that your spouse has died, and then there is the grief and sadness to cope with as well as the sudden aloneness.

Helen is in her forties and is divorced with two children. Helen feels that "it's not easy being single in any church". She recalls a time where she was effectively dropped from a house group after a decision was made to include spouses in the group – she didn't have a spouse, so no longer "fit" the group. She finds it difficult to walk into social events and gatherings on her own. She feels that as a single person she relies on God more and is able to have greater intimacy with God and in her prayer life. As a single parent there have been struggles financially, and also with not having another person to share the difficult decisions with. She says that she has tried to learn what Paul commends about being content in every circumstance.

Church – a place of safety or a place of judgment?

Some people I spoke to talked about feeling abandoned by their church while their marriage was in difficulty and while they were separating and divorcing. They felt that their married friends, and the church as a whole, simply didn't know what to do with them, how to react, or how to help. They found that married friends became wary of them after they became single again, and that invitations dried up. Some of the women felt that this was because their female friends were now suspicious of them being around their husbands. As we read in the story opposite, one told of being dropped from a house group that she had been part of for a long time, because the group changed to include spouses, and everyone else in the group was a couple. She was no longer welcome because she didn't fit.

Many spoke of struggling to find their place in church once they became single again, especially if they had children. All of a sudden there was no obvious social category for them to fit into – maybe they were too old for the young adults group, or couldn't make the events because of their children, but at the same time they felt that they no longer fitted into the family scene. For those who had children, the need for babysitters in order to attend any event or meeting meant that they often felt unable to join in with events that were happening.

This all has huge implications for the "single again" person. There are all the practical issues which may mean that you're unable to continue attending events or being part of groups that you were able to be part of before. On top of this is the experience of many people in this situation that suddenly people view and treat you differently to the way they did before, which can lead to you feeling isolated and excluded. It can feel as if you have been totally abandoned – not only has your marriage ended, but it also feels as though many friendships and relationships have ended, or changed beyond recognition.

There may be differences here too between the experiences of those who are widowed and those who are divorced. For those who are widowed, hopefully you will have found your close family, friends, and church community to have been supportive and helpful during your time of grief and loss. However, you may have found that such support was offered during the early stages, but was not sustained over a longer period of time, although your need for practical help and emotional support may have been just as great. For those who are divorced, there may have more uncertainty and embarrassment as to what people should say to you, or how they should respond to the situation. People may not have been fully aware of the circumstances involved and this may have led to painful or hurtful things being said. There is also the issue that in some churches, and for some Christians, divorce is very much disapproved of, and several of the divorced people I spoke to said that they had felt ostracized by Christian friends or within their church following their divorce.

One lady had, in contrast to many of the others, found her church to be very supportive of her during the time of her divorce. This church had managed to be a place of love and comfort at this very difficult time in her life. Later she and a friend had set up a social group within the church for divorced people, which many had found to be a great help. This group meets together to discuss the practical and emotional challenges of life after marriage. Sometimes they meet just as adults, and at other times with their children. Weekends can be lonely and tiring times, so sometimes they go out together then. The group has proved to be an easy place in which to welcome people who are not yet part of the church.

Gill is in her forties and a widow. Her church has quite a lot of single people in it and she enjoys the fact that there are often different social events going on. She values it when married people include her in their family life, but finds that because of their circumstances she's always expected to travel to visit them, rather than the other way around. She finds holidays and days off can be difficult, trying to plan in advance to see friends, and has just begun to think about retirement and about the different challenges that will bring.

What about the kids?

Some people who find themselves single again have children and some don't, and inevitably this has a big impact upon their experience of being single again. Where any young children are involved there will be a far greater effect on them, although with teenage and even adult children there can still be a big impact when a marriage ends. If you don't have children then it may be easier in some ways to slot back into the single life that you knew before you were married, since you are now entirely unattached once more. However, the flip side of this is that you may find yourself feeling very lonely now that you are completely on your own. Added to this there may be sadness at having no children, and perhaps a worry that you may never do so now that your marriage has ended.

For those who do have children, you now find yourself in a very different phase of life, as you are forced to work out what it means to be a single parent. You have to take on all the responsibilities of raising your children alone, which puts a huge financial, practical, and emotional burden upon you, and can feel like a very lonely situation to be in.

One person commented to me that when her children were young and she was struggling to bring them up alone, some of her friends whose spouses worked long hours or were not very hands-on as parents, would sometimes remark that they felt like single parents. She found this quite a hurtful comment since in reality they had no idea what life was like for her – they may have "felt like" single parents, but only she really was one.

Someone I spoke to made the comment that being divorced with children is a very different experience to having never been married, even though both do lead to "singleness". She felt that in some ways her situation was harder, since she has her daughter to care for and must face all the responsibilities alone, and finds it harder to socialize since she needs a babysitter. However, at the same time she felt that there were some parts of her situation that were better and easier – she has a child, which many single people would love to have, and she has someone she can go on holiday with, and who gives great hugs!

Win is in her sixties and is divorced with adult children. She feels accepted for who she is within her church, but doesn't feel that people really understand or appreciate the different challenges she faces as a single person. She would love people to offer practical help with jobs that need doing, but they never do! She has occasionally felt excluded from church events/services aimed at married couples, where there was no provision for single people, or no understanding that it might be difficult for them.

Considering remarriage?

Some people who find themselves single again will hope to remarry, while others will not want to. If you do want to, it may be even more difficult than for those who have never married. In some church circles remarriage after divorce is not seen as acceptable. If you have children there are many other factors to be taken into account when it comes to dating and possible remarriage, and it may be harder to meet people.

There were different views on this issue from the people I spoke to. One spoke of feeling a pressure from friends and the church to remarry – that somehow people would find it "easier" if she were to remarry, and that if she did so they would know what to do with her and how to treat her again. Another, however, felt that the pressure went the other way – that remarriage was frowned upon for theological reasons and therefore it was expected that after her divorce she would remain single, even though she longed to be married again.

Laura is in her fifties and divorced with three children. She has found it harder to fit in to her local church as a divorced person than she did when she was single before getting married. It's not so much that she feels unwelcome or unsupported in her local church, but rather she feels as though now she is single her friendships have changed, and it's harder to do things together because before her friends were mostly married couples. She finds relationships with married friends can sometimes be difficult because they are wary of her and there is a sense that suddenly she might interfere with their marriage in some way. Her most supportive friendships are with other single people, especially single parents, and many of these are from outside the church.

One issue which came up often is that the church simply doesn't know what to do in order to support divorced or widowed people. People often feel awkward around them and are not sure how to react or what to do. Earlier in the book we've looked at the issues single people face in our often "marriage-obsessed" church, and at the fact that there is very little teaching on singleness. However, several people who had found themselves single again felt that even the teaching that did take place was focused on those who had never married and were hoping to do so, and that this made them feel even more excluded.

Purely single

Clearly there are lots of ways in which being "single again" is different from being single for the first (or only) time. However, there are also a number of ways in which it is similar. All that has been written so far in this book – about the need for us to keep our eyes fixed on Jesus, to live full lives, and to remain pure – apply equally no matter who we are, or for how long we have been single.

It seems that everyone's experience is different when it comes to the question of living a celibate life after having been in a sexual relationship. From the questionnaire I carried out it did seem that those people who were divorced or widowed generally found living without sex harder than those who had never married. However, there are those who have never married who have nevertheless been in sexual relationships in the past, and so they would find it equally difficult. From the conversations I have had with people it appears that some feel that God has given them particular grace and has equipped them to be able to find living without sex less of a struggle; whereas for others it remains an ongoing area of struggle and difficulty.

Nevertheless, it's worth repeating that the goal for us all, as set out in the Bible, and commanded by God, is to live pure, holy lives with Jesus at the centre. Whether we have always been single or have been in a marriage that has ended; whether we are a virgin or have previously been in a sexual relationship; whether we hope to marry one day or are quite content as we are – if we are single, then we must be celibate. That's not necessarily going to be easy, of course, but it is the way that God calls us to live – holy and set apart for him. This is something that will be harder for some than for others. If this is the way in which you have chosen to live, then you may find it helpful to make yourself accountable to a close friend or a small group, and give them permission to ask you difficult and searching questions from time to time.

Tess is in her twenties and is divorced. She says that she doesn't think her singleness "has ever entered the consciousness" of her church. For her, singleness as a divorcee feels different to how it did before she was married. She values friendships with married people and finds them easier in some ways, as she can chat to and spent time with both partners, and stay over after a meal without any awkwardness. She also values friends who "share their children" with her. Tess says that she would find it very difficult to live on her own and so she has chosen to share a house with two others. She enjoys the freedom and flexibility of being single – in terms of what she does with her time, how she spends her money, and what decisions the makes. However, she finds it can be hard work arranging how to spend days off and holidays, and she misses having someone to "tell me everything will be OK and give me a hug".

Three different experiences of life after divorce...

Lisa's story

Lisa is in her forties and is divorced with a young daughter. She separated from her husband after they had been together for thirteen years, and married for ten. She has found becoming single again to be a huge change of identity, and has noticed how different it feels to be single now from how it felt when she was single for the first time.

When Lisa was in her early twenties and single, she was keen to find "the right person" and, although she lived a full life and enjoyed her independence, it was very important to her that she should settle down and get married. She feels that during this time other people related to her as "a woman who was waiting and searching for marriage". Her thoughts and dreams about the future all included the vision of a happy, romantic marriage.

When she met George and they began to date, a lot of things in her life began to change. She noticed that she spent more time with him than with her friends. Her main commitment was now to him and they began to make more and more decisions jointly – where to go on holiday, how to spend money, and so on. After they married she felt that her identity changed from "party girl" to "wife", and that "I" had now become "we" in all aspects of life.

After Lisa and George got married she noticed that relationships with other men also changed. In some ways they became easier because she was clearly attached and therefore "off limits", which meant that friendships could be simpler without wondering if there was more to it. However, in some ways they became harder since George was jealous of her friendships with men and so they had to be limited – again this was an identity change for her, as she had always had lots of male friends.

When Lisa and George divorced she found that a huge identity shift had to take place once more. She had to work out how to "be and understand" herself again as a single woman. She says, "Although the actual separation of things 'we' owned was relatively easy, it took me three years to work out what I actually liked and what I'd compromised on. Now I can really be me again, with my own style and interests. In a lot of ways it's been a journey of rediscovery of myself, and liberation – but even good journeys involve learning to see yourself and the world in a different way."

She has found that she has to rethink her relationships with men because initially she wasn't sure how to relate to them. Was she looking for another relationship? Were they interested in her? Did they view her differently because she was divorced? She has been working through this but finds that she can still feel self-conscious around men.

Lisa finds her local church to be very supportive of her, offering help with babysitting and other practical tasks. She also values the recognition there that being married isn't the only valid way of life as a Christian. However, she feels that there are issues within the wider church that are more difficult and she says she often feels "taken for granted" and "invisible" within the wider church.

One big issue for Lisa has been thinking about her future – she had always envisaged a future as part of a couple, but now she must make plans and preparations as a single person. Considering retirement and pensions as a single person is something that she finds quite scary.

Lisa has reflected that there is very little opportunity within the church for people who are divorced to reflect on their current circumstances. She says, "All the books about singleness are about those waiting to be married, and all the books about divorce are discussing whether or not it is appropriate for Christians to divorce and remarry." Neither of these speak into her situation, and she longs for some teaching to help her to make sense of what has happened, and also to work out how she should now live as Christian. She has also found that since some Christians are unable to accept divorce or remarriage, she sometimes isn't sure how people will react to her as a divorced Christian.

Her situation as someone who is "single again" but also has a child means that she can feel isolated within church. She says, "Despite the fact that we live in a society where divorce is common, as a Christian I am very much in the minority as a divorced woman. I rejoice with my friends and family, both single and married, but I do feel that as a single mum I don't have the freedom of a single woman [without children], or the live-in support of marriage. Spiritually the time since my divorce has had a lot of positives – my relationship with God (with the help of counselling and spiritual direction) is better than it has been for years, and this has come about as a result of my divorce. I have learned (well, sometimes, at least) to live in the present moment and to trust God to provide."

Simon's story

Simon is in his early thirties. He was married for seven years and has been divorced for two. He had always hoped to get married and had been in relationships since the age of seventeen. He is a sociable person who doesn't like to be on his own, so he enjoys the closeness and companionship of being in a relationship. He enjoyed being married, and was devastated when his wife left him because she'd had enough.

He found that he missed the closeness of marriage, and soon entered into another relationship, although he is currently single. He says, "Once you've had something and it's taken away, you feel like there's something missing. I guess you don't know what you've got till it's gone."

Simon is able now to see the mistakes that he made during his marriage and still carries the hurt of his failings. Although his wife walked out on him, he feels that if he had "just done better" as a husband then she would not have done so. He feels the pain of being divorced very strongly, and says that as a man and a husband he felt that he had a responsibility to lead his family. The fact that the marriage ended left him feeling like he had "failed in his most fundamental responsibility as a man".

When he and his wife separated his church supported him and not her, since she was the one who had initiated the split, whereas he had wanted to try to work things out. Later, however, they ceased to be supportive of him too. He feels that the people at his church had very much looked up to him and his wife and seen them as "the perfect couple". They were involved in various ministries and led a small group. After the divorce he felt that his identity

139

changed from one half of that perfect couple to "the single". Simon stopped serving in ministry and, since most of his close friendships were with people from church, at the same time as his marriage broke down he also lost most of his friends. He stopped getting invitations to people's houses, and they rarely accepted his invitations to spend time together.

Simon has since moved on and attends a different church. However, he stills feels that he has to somehow "justify" the fact that he is single and is sometimes quick to tell others that he used to be married. He often struggles to know who to be friends with. The largest population of singles are students, but he feels too old to be with them and believes that he doesn't quite fit into the same category as either the young married couples or the families. He feels that in relationships he has to make most of the effort.

He would like to get married again, but is nervous of "repeating his mistakes". The lessons he has learnt from his first marriage weigh on his mind and have left him with an awareness of the dedication and responsibility involved in being married.

Sally's story

Sally is in her fifties and is divorced with a teenage daughter. When she and her husband, Chris, separated, Sally and her daughter remained in their home, and Chris left. She has found that her *divorce has caused her to reflect on failure – was her marriage a "mistake" or something she and her husband had "failed" at? Initially dealing with the divorce was a private matter, but then it seemed to become public, with people telling her that it had an effect on them too – she reflects on the fact that, in the same way that a wedding is a very public declaration of love, a divorce can feel like a very public ending of that love.*

She has also felt herself to be judged to some extent by other Christians once she had "admitted" to being divorced. She knows herself to be a "forgiven sinner", but for some Christians her divorce has seemed to be unforgivable.

Sally has noticed that she feels differently about being single now from how she felt before she was married. Before, she hoped to be married and have children, but it wasn't the "be all and end all of life". However, finding herself single again at this point in her life, she feels as though people view her singleness as "less than being part of a couple". She has also noticed that she finds ticking the box marked "divorced" on a questionnaire much harder than she ever found ticking the box marked "single". Of course, she recognizes that she doesn't know what it would feel like to have always been single.

She has been saddened by the impact that her divorce has had on her daughter, and on her daughter's relationship with Chris, but recognizes that this is not something that she can "fix". She is able to discuss parenting issues with him, but only after the fact, meaning that all major decisions have to be taken by herself, which can be hard. They decided that the three of them would get together at Christmas and birthdays – this was best for their daughter but was personally very difficult for Sally. All of Sally's time since the divorce has been taken up with looking after her daughter, and with work: "There is no time for oneself (at all, whatsoever)."

She found friends, family, neighbours, and church to be very supportive, offering love, care, and practical help such as babysitting. She was grateful to those who encouraged her "to continue to be the person I am and not to let the divorce take too much away from me". However, some were a bit too supportive – wanting her to go out and celebrate the divorce. In fact, Sally describes the day her decree absolute came through as "the saddest day of my life".

Sally hasn't really thought about future relationships, though people often tell her that she is bound to meet someone some day (and she wishes that they wouldn't!). She says that "I always felt complete in myself as a single person before marriage, and I feel complete in myself now; my faith has always meant that I know to whom I belong and, although I may be lonely at times, this has never led to me wanting to be in a relationship." Her daughter is *her priority and she isn't sure how a new relationship would really work, or fit into their lives.*

She has found the question of holidays to be an issue since her divorce – her daughter is now at an age where she wants to go away with friends, and all of her own friends go away with their families, which makes working out holiday plans very difficult. Having said that, she doesn't have any problem fitting in with or socialising with friends and with people she meets, whether they are single or married.

Bev's thoughts

Bev has written about her divorce in her book Created as a Woman.[1] *One day she sensed that Jesus was calling her to "arise". Not understanding what this meant, she searched the commentaries and found the word "arise" defined as to "come back to life". Bev realized that the pain of her divorce had caused her to unconsciously protect her heart – not allowing herself to be hurt in the same way again. This meant that her heart had become "anaesthetized"; numbed not only to pain but also to fullness of joy. Jesus, however, wanted more for her than this – he was truly calling her to come back to life.*

As Jesus continued to speak to her heart and to call her to "arise", Bev wrote the following poem, which she has given me permission to reproduce here:

Divorce: *Our marriage is handed to the solicitors and left*
        to die
        Lots are cast for our belongings and money
        divided between us
        People stare or gloat, saying knowingly that
        they had expected it.
        This is divorce.

Divorce: *I walk through the ordinariness of life*
        But my very being is out of joint and my heart
        melted within me.
        I am wounded deeply and my strength has dried
        up — poured out in a pretence of normality.
        This is divorce.

Divorce: *My tomb has been of my choosing*
        The protective rock feels so safe
        My cold flesh an anaesthetic against pain
        The darkness a cover for my woundedness and
        shame
        The stone, my defence against life.

Lord: *You stand outside my tomb*
        You shake with anger at my torment
        You weep with grief at my pain and loss
        You order the stone to be rolled away.

Light enters the darkness and I am afraid — vulnerable.
I cower in a corner — can I face the crowd?

You command me to come out and my feet obey, yet I tremble.
Gentle hands remove my grave clothes – gone are my defences.
I am "let go" from all that bound me.

What now O Lord?
I stand before you torn – torn between the longing for the
*   safety of my tomb*
And the delicious feeling of the sun, the fresh air
*   – of life itself.*
I cannot go back, for I am alive again!
I cannot choose darkness when you are in the light.
And so I walk away from my empty tomb
I put my hand in yours and choose life.

Not just single, but single again

Whatever circumstances of life we find ourselves in, Jesus is right there in the midst of it with us. We're reminded in Deuteronomy that "The Lord himself goes before you and will be with you; he will never leave you nor forsake you. Do not be afraid; do not be discouraged."[2]

That's true in all parts of our life, all the time. It's true when we struggle with being single, and it's true when we find ourselves unexpectedly, and perhaps unhappily, single again.

I discussed all this with a friend recently and at the end of our conversation she said this sentence, which I think pretty much sums it up: "Jesus is still trustworthy, even when we have baggage!"

Chapter 6

Living together

Writing to the Christians in Corinth, Paul uses the metaphor of the human body to describe how the church is supposed to function:

> Just as a body, though one, has many parts, but all
> its many parts form one body, so it is with Christ.
> For we were all baptized by one Spirit so as to form
> one body – whether Jews or Gentiles, slave or free
> – and we were all given the one Spirit to drink.
> Even so the body is not made up of one part but
> of many. Now if the foot should say, "Because I am
> not a hand, I do not belong to the body," it would
> not for that reason stop being part of the body...
> If the whole body were an eye, where would the
> sense of hearing be? If the whole body were an ear,
> where would the sense of smell be? But in fact God
> has placed the parts in the body, every one of them,
> just as he wanted them to be. If they were all one
> part, where would the body be? As it is, there are

many parts, but one body. The eye cannot say to
the hand, "I don't need you!" And the head cannot
say to the feet, "I don't need you!" On the contrary,
those parts of the body that seem to be weaker
are indispensable, and the parts that we think are
less honourable we treat with special honour. And
the parts that are unpresentable are treated with
special modesty, while our presentable parts need
no special treatment. But God has put the body
together, giving greater honour to the parts that
lacked it, so that there should be no division in the
body, but that its parts should have equal concern
for each other. If one part suffers, every part suffers
with it; if one part is honoured, every part rejoices
with it. Now you are the body of Christ, and each
one of you is a part of it.[1]

We see then that the church is supposed to function like a
body, with every part equally valid, used, and respected.
Church should be a place where everyone feels valued and
able to use their gifts and skills to contribute to the whole. It
should be a place where everyone receives a welcome and is
accepted just as they are, while being lovingly challenged to
become the best possible version of themselves.

Church at its best really does work in this way, and when
that happens it's beautiful. But of course churches are human
institutions made up of human people, and so things don't
always work as they are supposed to. The people who make
up church congregations, and the people who lead them, are

sinners who mess up on a very regular basis. Often we hurt and offend each other entirely without meaning to when we say and do things that are unkind, unthinking, or insensitive. Sometimes we find it difficult to imagine ourselves in the shoes of our brother or sister, and so we make assumptions about their lives. Sometimes we are envious of what they have and we don't have. Sometimes we ignore or overlook them because we think we have nothing in common and we don't know what to say to them.

Often when I speak to single people I find that they mention things their married brothers and sisters have said or done that have hurt and upset them. And yet it is also true that as single people we sometimes hurt and upset our married friends. Sadly too often, instead of raising these issues and using them as an opportunity to learn about one another's lives and to strengthen our relationships, we keep quiet and allow the hurt to fester.

The idea behind this chapter is to begin a dialogue between single people and married people; to allow each group to say to the other some of the things they have longed to say, but also to really listen, patiently and graciously, to one another, and to be prepared where necessary to learn and to change.

My hope is that everyone reading this will be encouraged to think about what they say and how they say it, as well as to consider how their words might be heard and felt by others. Where it's necessary for us to change the way we speak, I hope that we will have the grace to do that.

Steve is in his forties and has never been married. He doesn't feel that his church is "discriminatory" against him as a single person, but that they just didn't really do anything to "positively support" him as a single person. He has married friends who include him in their plans and activities, but he finds that many of them try to "fix" his singleness. Since most of them have children, he generally has to fit around their plans, and while he is happy to do that for most of the time, he would like it if they were sometimes willing to compromise a bit more and do things with him just as adults. The thing he enjoys most about being single is the freedom and independence it brings; however he misses having a close relationship that challenges him to see who he really is. He feels that "community" is key, and that "the church does a better job at community than most other places, but we still don't do it very well".

Sometimes it's best not to say anything at all...

So here, as we begin, is my top ten list of things single people wish married people wouldn't say to them...

1. You're so lovely, why are you still single?

This is quite a favourite, it seems – I have lost count of the number of people who have said it to me, or about others in my hearing. On the face of it you might wonder what's wrong with it – surely it's meant as a compliment? Well, yes, I'm sure that it is *meant* as a compliment. The problem is that when that sentence is spoken, this is what I hear: "You *seem* lovely, but there must be something wrong with you, otherwise you'd be married. You can't be quite as lovely as all the lovely married people around you. If you were only a bit *more* lovely, you'd be married in no time." I know, I know, that's not what you meant at all – but unfortunately that is what I heard.

2. Don't worry, you're still so young.

This is another tricky one, because on the face of it it's complimentary, and it seems to offer consolation and hope. But to be brutally honest, when you say this sentence I simply cannot hear you over the sound of my biological clock ticking. I have known people aged sixteen and aged sixty who felt exactly the same about their desire to be married (and of course I have also known people at both of those ages, and everywhere in between, who had no desire whatsoever to be married). At the moment when singleness feels like a struggle, whatever age you are, you don't ever feel young enough to not worry about it.

3. Do you have a family?

I mentioned this favourite of mine back in chapter one. I wish I had a pat reply to this question that worked every time but sadly, for some reason, no matter how many times I get asked it, I still stumble over my response. Don't get me wrong, I have no problem with the questions "Are you married?" or "Have you got children?" Those are questions seeking information that are perfectly valid in a conversation, and to which I'm quite happy to reply. But the question above isn't the same as those questions. The question above means "Are you married with children?", but that isn't what it asks, and so we find ourselves thrown by it. I find it hard to answer because the answer is yes, I do have a family – I have parents and grandparents, aunts and uncles, and cousins. But I know that's not what you're really asking. If I reply in that way you might think I'm being deliberately obtuse, and that's not what I want to do. And yet I don't want to say "no" because that isn't the right answer to the question you have asked, even if it is the right answer to the question that you meant. Can you see why it's confusing?

4. If you get your relationship with God sorted out, then he'll send you a spouse.

This is clearly nonsense! What more needs to be said? So presumably absolutely every married Christian person has a perfectly healthy, mature relationship with God then, do they? No, that's what I thought...

5. I was single till the age of X, so I know exactly how you feel.

I'm sorry, but you simply don't. It's obviously true that while not everyone is married at some point in their lives, everyone is single at some point. But you don't know how I feel. You may of course be able to remember how being single felt for you, at that time, but that is not the same as how it feels for me, now. In the same way, I don't know how anyone else feels – even another thirty-four-year-old single female vicar. (This doesn't mean that you can't empathize, or sympathize, or be involved in my life – of course it doesn't. But you really don't know how I feel.)

6. Do you think maybe you're being too picky?

Ah yes, that'll be it. When I looked out at that queue of seventeen men beating each other off with sticks to get to me first, and then rejected each of them in turn, it was my pickiness that was the problem.

7. Have you thought about speed dating/internet dating/blind dating?

Dating? You mean I could be looking for men to date? Wow – I had no idea, thank goodness you told me. It's not like I've been wrestling for months over whether or not this is a road to go down, and how, why, when, and where it might all happen, and what I'll do if it doesn't work out. I'll get onto that straight away.

8. You're so lucky to be footloose and fancy free.

Yes, you're right, I am. I'm really lucky to have freedom in where I go, what I do, and how I spend my time and my money. It's great to be able to be independent and to make my own decisions. But you're really lucky to have someone to hug when you get home at night, someone to share the household chores with, someone to talk through your day with, and someone to go to parties with. And if in the context of our friendship we can talk about the things that are great for me and the things that are great for you, and share them together, along with the things that are hard for us both, then that's brilliant. But if you throw the above sentence at me when I'm feeling lonely and alone then I will find it hard to be gracious.

9. My husband/wife/children are driving me mad. It's so hard being married/having children – if I were you I wouldn't bother.

So would you like to swap places? No, I thought not. Please don't insult me and your family with this one. You're allowed to have a bad day, week, or month. We all are. And if there's one thing I don't envy parents it's sleepless nights. But please, don't say things you don't mean.

10. I think God has given me a word for you – you'll be married by the age of X/be pregnant by next Christmas/have six children...

I hardly know what to say about this one. I wholeheartedly believe in prayer and prophecy, and I love to give and be given words from God – it's a joy and a privilege. But please, please, please DON'T give people words about marriage and children, no matter how positively sure you are that God has spoken. If need be, write the word down, seal it in an envelope, and hide it away – if it comes true, take it out and give it to the person. It will be a wonderful confirmation from God. But refrain from saying it to them. I guarantee that it will not be helpful. Ever.

Clearly that was all a bit tongue-in-cheek! But the sentences themselves were all real – all things that I or my friends have had said to us; all things which have been found hurtful and painful; all things which we'd really rather not have said to us again.

So what do we do then? Do we decide that friendships between married people and single people can't ever really work, since our life circumstances are so different, and conclude that we'd all be better off not bothering? Of course not. For one thing, I think that churches are meant to be heterogeneous – they are meant to contain a mixture of people of different genders, ages, backgrounds, and life circumstances. We're all meant to work out how to get on together and be family.

Barbara is in her sixties and has never married. She has no children of her own, but enjoys being a godmother and a "second mum" to a number of people. She feels very supported by her church, which makes sure single people are included in all events and activities. Her church has put on various different relationship events, which have included teaching sessions for single people. She has valued such events, and other teaching she has heard, because it has been honest about both the joys and the challenges of being single. She values her friendships with married friends who are "just interested in me as a person", but she feels that sometimes they can be unaware of how it feels to have to come home to an empty house and to have no one with whom to share experiences or emotions. She also thinks that people sometimes imagine that single people are very self-sufficient and capable, whereas this may not always be the case.

155

In the questionnaire I sent out to single friends, I asked how many of them had close married friends with whom they could share life. The overwhelming majority said that they had such friendships, which were a blessing to them. Here are some of the ways in which people said that these friendships worked well:

- When they invite me to be part of their family, including me in everyday events as well as special occasions, making me feel welcome in their homes, and allowing me access to their children's lives.

- When they offer me practical help with things that are difficult to do by myself, such as house, garden, and car maintenance.

- When they treat me as an equal friend, rather than as someone in a lesser state than them who is to be pitied and looked after.

- When they look out for me to make sure that I'm safe and can get home late at night.

- When they don't treat my singleness as an unmentionable issue, but ask me how I feel about it and if I'm OK with it (but at the same time don't make it the only thing we ever talk about!).

- When they invite me round on my own, rather than feeling that they also need someone else there to make up the numbers so we're all couples.

- When they make me feel welcome and at ease in their home, not as if I'm in the way or intruding.

- When they make sure I'm not alone at significant times like birthdays, Christmas, Easter, and New Year's Eve.

- When they're willing to listen and act as a sounding board when I've got big decisions to make.

- When they invite me to eat with them, both on special occasions and also on ordinary days.

- When I'm able to sometimes spend time with just one of them on their own rather than always being part of a three.

- When they're open and honest and talk about their marriage in a balanced way.

- When they avoid being overly physically intimate when I'm there, so that I don't feel awkward.

- When they pray for me and with me, and ask what I'd like them to pray for rather than assuming they know.

- When they invite me to go on holidays with them.

- When they give me hugs (and allow their children to do the same!).

I love all these! What beautiful examples of how relationships between married people and single people can not only work but flourish and be life-enhancing for everyone involved.

Mary is in her sixties. She values the various social and networking opportunities that are available to her within her church; however, she finds that there isn't a culture of hospitality being offered within people's own homes. Rather than separate teaching/events for single people, she would like to see the more varied and diverse issues of the whole church community addressed together, and values the mutuality which is present in the body of Christ. She values the times when she can talk and pray with married friends but finds that (not unreasonably!) she is "ditched" during times of stress, since the person naturally turns to their spouse in those times. She recognizes that many of the things she has done in her life would not have been possible had she married, saying: "The sacrifices I have made have been more than compensated by what has been made possible as a result."

As you might expect, however, there were also some negatives expressed – ways in which married people act that aren't helpful to single people. Here are some of those:

- When they try to be matchmakers for me without my permission.

- When they act as a couple in ways that feel excluding and uncomfortable (this may be overt shows of affection, or it may be having big arguments).

- When they don't really understand what my life is like.

- When I always have to fit in round them, so whenever we meet it has to be on their terms.

- When they use me as a babysitting service.

- When they only invite me round at certain times, but save the "special times" like Saturday nights for their married friends.

- When they talk non-stop about their children.

- When they moan about their children without realizing that I would love to have what they have.

- When friends, who have been very close while they were single, disappear when they get married and don't keep in touch.

- When they assume that because I don't have children I don't want to be included in their family events.

- When they assume that I am self-sufficient and capable all of the time, and don't need any help or support.

- When they ditch me during times of stress in their lives because they turn instead to their family (understandably), and I feel shut out.

- When they don't ever invite me to join them for holidays.

This is a very interesting list. The first thing that strikes me is that it's slightly shorter than the list of positives. I think some of these things are really a case of us all needing to be open and honest, and to express how we're feeling. We can't expect other people to be mind readers and to know that we're upset, and why. Most people are kind, caring, and compassionate (at least most of the time!). If they realize that they have been acting in ways that have hurt us then they will be very sorry and they will want to stop. We need to be able to express ourselves honourably and graciously, and to look at ways in which we can move our relationship forwards.

Babysitting featured on that list – it's an interesting topic! For most of my adult life I have cheerfully volunteered to babysit for friends with children. It's something I enjoy, especially if the children are still awake when I arrive and I can play with them before they go to bed and get a goodnight cuddle! When I was at university and college it struck me as an excellent thing to do as often as possible, since the families in question generally had much nicer houses than me, with bigger TVs and more food to eat. However, I also know plenty of single friends who cannot think of a worse way to spend their evening than babysitting, and would probably be offended to even be asked. So it's definitely a personal thing.

I have had some contrasting experiences where babysitting is concerned. I was once invited to the home of some friends for dinner. Or so I thought. When I arrived, dressed up and clutching a bottle of wine, I was met with two very distracted people clearly in a rush. As they left the house, they called instructions behind them about the children, the TV, and the dinner they had left me. I have no idea how the misunderstanding had occurred, but while I thought I was going round to spend the evening with them, they thought that they had invited me to babysit. It was all very embarrassing for me, but I don't think they ever realized that I was expecting a very different sort of evening.

In contrast to that was a time at college when some friends asked me to babysit and I agreed. They said that they would leave me a meal, and kindly asked me what foods I was particularly missing because they weren't provided in our somewhat limited college fare. I began to list some of them – interesting bread, nice cheese, grapes, fresh salad... Before I knew it I was in a gastronomic daydream and they had got rather more of an answer than they had bargained for. I had almost forgotten about this conversation when I turned up at their house, but they hadn't. They presented me with a huge tray containing every single item I had mentioned. It was far more than even I could eat in one meal. When I left they wrapped everything up for me to take home. What an extraordinarily generous thing to do!

There were other friends who would bring a home-baked cake in as a gift for whoever had babysat for them over the weekend; and still others who would invite all the single students around for meals during the term so that we didn't feel that the only time we visited their home was to babysit. Everyone in the equation was blessed – the married couples who got to have time to themselves; the children who got to spend time with different, fun adults; and the single people who got to share a little in "family" life.

James is in his forties and has never married. He values his friends who are married with children and invite him to become part of their lives and to join in with day to day family life. However, he finds that sometimes friends can "disappear" when they get married, and only want to spend time with other married people; or that the friendship dynamic can change so that the relationship feels very different. He finds that people don't always know how to "handle" him as a single person, and tend to see his singleness as a problem that needs to be fixed. He also wishes there were more single people in church, who could be looked up to as role models to show that it is possible to live a happy and fulfilled single life. He sees the biggest benefit of being single as the freedom it brings; but the hardest part is not being part of a ready-made unit.

Married people strike back...

Above I've mentioned things that single people would like married people not to say, as well as things married people do which are or aren't helpful. So it's time the married people had their say. I've spoken to some friends, and here are some of the things they would like single people to know:

- Marriage is really hard! It takes time, effort, energy, compromise, forgiveness, and grace. It can be fantastic some, or even most, of the time, but it doesn't just happen – it takes a lot of hard work.

- Marriage is nothing like you think it's going to be, and you can't be totally prepared for it. If you're expecting marriage to solve all your problems and to provide you with someone who will always listen to you at the end of a hard day, do all the household chores that you can't, completely satisfy your sex drive, and provide you with the children you long for… then beware. These are some of the good things that may come out of marriage, but they are not guaranteed.

- Sex is nothing like it is in the movies!

- When I talk about the difficulties and stresses of being married or having children, I don't do it order to hurt you because you don't have them. I do it to try to make you feel happier in your own situation, and because I care about you.

- If you're not OK on your own, you're not going to be OK when you get married. That doesn't mean "get yourself sorted and your spouse will instantly and miraculously appear". But it does mean that you shouldn't put off dealing with character and discipleship issues in the belief that everything will be alright once you're married.

- I'm aware of the needs my single friends have, and the pressures they are going through, and I really want to help and support them. However, keeping my marriage on track, and looking after my kids, takes up so much of my time that sometimes I don't manage to be there for my single friends in the way that I would like to. It isn't that I don't care or understand.

- Marriage may start with romance but it only lasts the course with a lot of hard work, sacrifice, and self-giving. At times you may not even like things about the person you have promised to love. To make it last is really hard work.

- We don't want to feel guilty for being happy or that we need to hide it from you. Sometimes it feels as though we daren't mention any of the great things about being married for fear of upsetting you – but we don't want to upset you, we simply want to share the good things in our lives with you.

- We'd love to socialize with you. We realize there can be obstacles to overcome from both sides – childcare, time to prepare, space to host, and so on – but we'd love to try to work out a compromise together.

- When we got married I found that it was exciting planning our wedding day and organizing everything, but then after the big day there was a time when friends didn't contact me so much anymore. It was as if people thought we needed total space together, whereas in reality life still goes on and I needed my friends as much as I ever did. So single people – when your friends get married, please still ring, text, and email. We don't want to be cut-off – we still need you.

- We need friends besides our spouse for our own sanity! There's no way that one person can provide absolutely every emotional and spiritual need that I have. I still need other friends to laugh, cry, and pray with. That's part of who I am, so I really value having a few close friends who

I know will always be there for me. Whether they're single or married doesn't really come into it, they're just friends.

- I've found that as I've got older I'm more and more aware of other people's sensitivities and what they've got to deal with. When we got married, I may have not been as sensitive as I could have been to how single friends may have felt at our wedding. Also, when we had children I know I said and did things in my joyfulness that hurt a couple of friends who were either childless or struggling to have children. I guess the point is that I want to apologize, but also say that it's really hard to know where the line is sometimes. I want my friends to be able to be joyful with me when I'm joyful but without hurting them in the process – so please tell me if I overstep that line; I'd rather know so that I can do better next time.

- I'd like to say to my single friends, please invite me for evenings out/in just with you. The biggest thing I miss since getting married is evenings with friends. The fact that I'm married doesn't mean that you have to invite my spouse to everything too.

- The fact that a couple are going out/married doesn't mean they're literally joined at the hip. This doesn't happen so much anymore, but when we were first going out people used to assume we had to sit next to each other in church, or in the pub, or wherever, and would move out of the way so we could do so. We can still function as individuals even if we're part of a couple. Please let me be me as a person as well as a spouse!

Orla is in her forties and has always been single. At her church she has heard teaching specifically about singleness and community, which she has found helpful. She also finds it a caring and supportive place. She feels loved and supported by her married friends, but isn't sure that they fully understand what life is like for her as a single person. She values the fact that they include her in their lives and in their plans. Sometimes, though, this can feel as if she is the one who always has to travel to visit them, or always has to fit in with their plans. The hardest thing for her about never getting married has been not having children. She says, "Being married is a choice, being single often isn't – and that can lead to frustration and regret."

Building relationships is always worth it

So the married people have had their say – now it's me writing again. And I want to say to all of us as single people that we should try to cultivate friendships with married people and families, because it will enhance and enrich our lives so much. At the same time, we need to recognize that their lives are very different from our own. There will be times when compromise is needed. There will be times when it will feel as though much of the "give" is coming from us. We may often have to be the one who goes to visit them, because if they have children it's so much easier for it to happen that way. We will need to respect their boundaries – their need for couple and family time that doesn't include us; their need for some days off and holidays alone; their need for bedtimes and routines to be observed. But it will be worth it a hundredfold for all that we will receive in return.

We need to beware, though, that we don't collude with the false image I mentioned back in chapter two, of single people not being quite "grown up". If we're not careful, we can fall into this trap – expecting the married people to always invite the single people round and falling into a parent/child relationship. This is neither helpful nor healthy. Relationships between married and single people are equal – both sides have something to give and something to gain. Maybe as single people we will have to do more of the travelling to visit our married friends, especially if they have small children. However, we can also invite them round sometimes, or offer to cook at their house, or arrange picnics or family outings. One of the highlights of my year is a Christmas party I put on one Saturday afternoon in December. An ever-growing crowd of people gather – there are single people, married people, and families, and I love to host them all and provide lots of cake and other goodies.

I am blessed to have a few very good friendships with married couples, a number of whom have small children. These friendships bring so much to my life. I get a different perspective than I would have if all of my friends were also single. I get to join in with family life sometimes – being there for everyday meal times, going on the school run, doing the bathtime and bedtime routine. This is a joy and brings something to my life that otherwise I would never experience.

It also sometimes makes me extremely grateful to get back to my quiet, uncluttered house!

I love being able to be part of the lives of my friends' children – being "Aunty Kate" is one of the biggest joys of my life, especially because as an only child I have no "real" nieces or nephews. I love the relationship I have with these children. They regularly inform anyone who will listen that I am part of their family – I get drawn on family portraits and mentioned in family prayers. They confide in me, share their lives with me, and hug me, and it's amazing! I know that as they get older our relationship will change, but it will continue to be just as wonderful, as they grow and mature, and I become a trusted adult who they can talk to about life and love and faith. What a blessing that is.

Sometimes, if I'm honest, it's hard to have this level of relationship. It's a joy, but it comes with a cost as well. Having a glimpse into family life is a huge blessing but it also reminds me of what I don't have. However, the blessings far outweigh the costs. It is *so* worth it.

The relationships that I have with married couples work well for a number of reasons. It's interesting to note that most of my closest married friends are people whom I have met as couples, or if not, then I met both partners at about the same time as they met each other. I certainly don't think that it's impossible to be close friends with someone, then for them to get married and for that friendship to extend to their spouse, but I do think it's harder and that the relationship will have a slightly different dynamic. Another factor I think is that in all cases I have a friendship with both the man and woman in the couple. I think this is really important, because it means that I can easily spend time with the whole family. Where the couple have children I also have a very good relationship with them, although in most cases I knew the couple before they had children.

The relationships also work well because of the respect, grace, and give and take that happens. I know that if we have something planned and one of the children is ill or the babysitter cancels then we'll have to rearrange. I know that most of the time I'll have to visit their house rather than they mine. I also know that they'll always be there for me if something big happens in my life or if I just need someone to talk to.

With my closest friends, Mike and Kate Hindley, we have found a pattern that works for me and for them. Fortunately we only live about ten minutes apart, which makes things much easier. They invite me round for special meals after the children have gone to bed, and also for everyday teatimes with the children. Usually we meet at their house, but they recognize that sometimes I like to host so they make the effort to come to me too. I go to their house for breakfast every Christmas morning because they understand that that's a difficult time to be alone. They let me blather on about my work and my life because they know that as an extrovert who lives alone sometimes I just need to talk! When the three of us are going out with other friends, sometimes they'll pick me up so that I can have a drink and I don't have to go into the party on my own. I'm happy to babysit because I know that they don't expect it but really appreciate it. I know that they'll make plans with me for my birthday and make sure that I have a cake.

Recently, I started an eighteen-month leadership course that began with a Saturday for participants and "supporters". For everyone on the course except me, that meant a spouse. I wanted Kate to come with me but hadn't actually asked her because I assumed that she wouldn't be able to due to family commitments. It was actually Mike who suggested that she come with me, and offered to change around his own work and diary commitments so that she was free to come. We haven't got to this point without some effort and adjustments – we've known each other for ten years – but I think I can say that all three adults and three children in the equation are better off as a result of our friendship.

Often I have spoken to single people who have been hurt by something a married person has said to them, or who have found friendships with married people too difficult to sustain, and so have chosen instead to only pursue deep friendships with other single people. I think this is a real shame. When single and married people, those with children, and younger and older people are friends, everyone involved benefits. We all learn to compromise, we all have our horizons broadened, we all have an opportunity to grow in grace – and we may just have some fun along the way.

Chapter 7

Happily ever after...

If this were a child's fairytale book, it would end with the words "and they all lived happily ever after." That's how all the best books finish, right? But real life just isn't like that – or is it? Well, maybe, just maybe, it is. Or at least, it could be.

When we live life with God, that's the best possible life, the "happily ever after" life. Don't get me wrong, I'm not being naive – I know only too well that being a Christian doesn't mean that we won't go through hard times, or that we won't have struggles in our lives. But when we have chosen to live our lives God's way then that will be the best possible life. You see, in a very real way, God is all we need.

Now, let me unpack that a bit more, because I know that some of you will have already started to mutter and grumble about that last sentence! Often we feel like the apocryphal little girl whose story is told in so many sermon illustrations – when her dad goes to tuck her into bed one night, she tells him that she is scared to be alone in the dark. Her dad tells her that she doesn't need to be scared because God is with her. The little girl thinks about this for a moment and then says, "But Daddy, I want someone with skin on." I don't know about you, but in the times of pain and loneliness, I too "want someone with skin on."

So what does it mean for us to say that God is all we need? I've been reflecting on this over the past year or so. It first began when I noticed that quite a few of the worship songs I was listening to and singing contained a line that in some way proclaimed that God is all we need. I don't like to say or sing something if I don't really mean it, so I found myself thinking about this concept What did it mean? Was it true for me? If so, what would that look like? And if not, was it something that I should be aiming for?

I guess that in the end my answer to the question "Is God all I need?" was both yes and no. What a wonderful Christian compromise! Yes, in the sense that God is everything to me – he made me, he has always been with me, he loves me, he is interested in my life, he longs to spend time with me, he speaks to me. Several years ago a wise Christian leader introduced me to the writings of Julian of Norwich.[1] I have always loved the story of Julian reflecting on a hazelnut that she held in her hand, and on how awesome the God must be who could make such a thing. As she looked at it she spoke these words: "God made it, God loves it, God will keep it. God is my Maker, my Lover and my Keeper." Julian understood something that we would all do well to understand – that God is everything to us, all that we need, and so much more besides.

And yet I am absolutely certain that we are not meant to exist in isolation. Just as I believe it is very difficult (although, of course, possible) to be a Christian and not go to church, I also believe that it is very difficult (although, again, possible) to be a human being and not be in relationship with others, in a family or community of some sort. And I don't think that this is just something God allows or tolerates because he knows that we're a bit hopeless and not quite able to manage on our own. No, I believe that community is something God-ordained and precious.

Ever since God declared that it was "not good" for Adam to be alone,[2] human beings have been living alongside one another, sharing life together. I need other people in my life. I need them to offload to after a bad day; I need them to work alongside me in ministry; I need them to share a bottle of wine with me as we put the world to rights; I need them to point out to me the parts of my character that need working on; I need them to celebrate with me when good things happen; I need them to spend my days off and holidays with; I need them to give me a hug and tell me that everything's going to be OK.

So is God all I need? Well, yes... and no. I think in the end what I want to say is that God is all I need, but he doesn't want to be all I have. It isn't wrong to want and need the company and friendship of others; it is only wrong if that need becomes an idol to us, and if we become dependent on other people to meet all of our needs. God should be the one on whom we depend, and to whom we turn first of all in good times and bad.

So today, I say or sing the words "God is all I need" and I really mean them. I know that there will be times when I'm surrounded by people I love, life is good, and God will be in the centre of it all. And I know too that there will be times

173

when I feel lonely, lost and afraid, when life is hard, and I will need to cling on to God. But in the midst of it all, in the most important way, he is all that I need.

I need to remind myself of this, because I can be slow to catch on and then quick to forget. I'm fortunate to live in a lovely big vicarage, so I'm able to have a "prayer room", which I just love. On one of the walls I have a number of mirror tiles, and I have written certain words on the tiles, so that every time I look in the mirror I remember certain truths that God speaks over me. The words say precious, transformed, saved, redeemed, blessed, freed, forgiven, accepted, justified, chosen, loved, and sent. This is who I am. These are the truths I need in my life. When I can remember those truths, then the other things all fit into place much more easily.

You see, my acceptance, affirmation, and worth (and yours) need to come from God, and only from God. When we look to him for those things, and when we are able to receive them from him, we are on our way to living full and whole lives. When we look to other people for those things, we will look in vain. If we spend our lives on hold, waiting and searching for the perfect someone who will bring us all those things and more, we will only end up being disappointed. (Please don't imagine that I have got this all neatly sorted out in my life – it's something I think we all need to continually work on, and of which we need to remind ourselves regularly.)

Jo Saxton reminds us that Jesus showed us how to live the best possible life of all – and he was single:

We know that God designed marriage and that when marriages work, transformed by his love and grace, they are powerful and influential. We also know Jesus modelled how to live an unmarried God-filled life with meaningful friendships and a powerful impact on the people He came into contact with. Whatever our marital status, life with Jesus means life to the full. Yet Jesus warns that our enemy will continually seek to undermine a fulfilled and purposeful life in Christ. And so as far as the battle is concerned: It. Is. On.[3]

Being single – the fantastic bits!

When I questioned some of my friends on how they felt about being single, lots of the same points came up again and again. There were lots of positives that people identified – the things we love about being single. Here is a reminder of some of the positives we have already looked at, along with a few extra ones:

- Being able to decide on and do things spontaneously
- Having to face up to my own character issues and deal with them
- Having to totally rely on God
- Learning how to do practical jobs
- Having freedom to spend lots of time with God
- Pleasing myself about what I eat and drink

- Having freedom to make my own plans and decisions
- Being able to take on new roles and responsibilities as I choose
- Flexibility about how I use my time
- No one to shout at me if I bump the car!
- Developing self confidence, such as being able to go into parties and pubs alone
- Choosing my own style of house and garden decor
- Being able to be generous with money
- Being able to serve and give out more – no one will need me later at home, so I can just come in and rest
- Building intimate friendships
- Being able to choose times of solitude
- Lower cost of living
- Being able to be hospitable and keep an open house
- Taking holidays in school time

(Someone also added "staying young-looking – at least if you don't have kids" – it's worth considering that one as a plus too!)

What a great list that is! It's useful to take time to remember all of the really great things about being single, the things that we value and enjoy. We know that is not the whole story, and there's another list coming in a moment. But it is so important that we recognize and acknowledge all of the great things we have the opportunity to do if we are single. Lots of married people would read the list above and be extremely envious of all of those opportunities and possibilities that are available to us because we are single. Admittedly, they're not all given to us on a plate – some of them we have to reach out and grab, or work hard for – but they are all potential advantages and benefits for those of us who are single, so let's make the most of them!

Being single – the difficult bits

The people I spoke to also identified some of the more difficult aspects of being single, and it is important to acknowledge some of the challenges we have considered. Here is the list of things people found harder, or thought were possible risks:

- Becoming selfish and set in your ways

- Becoming too independent (as opposed to interdependent, which is a positive thing)

- Coming home to an empty house

- Feeling lonely

- Not necessarily being as devoted to God as I could be – spending as much time wrestling with being single as my married friends spend with their families!

- No one to care for me if I'm ill

- No one with whom to share dreams and decision making

- Eating and drinking alone

- Lack of physical contact and hugs

- No one with whom to have a laugh

- No one to point out and help me to work on my bad habits

- Struggling with practical jobs

- Other people viewing me in a certain way (feeling as if I am a "social failure")

- No one to make me take time off

- Not feeling loved and cherished by anyone

- Cost of living is more

- Having to do all the chores

- Worrying about the future – planning for retirement and facing old age alone

- No one with whom to celebrate significant life events (who makes me a birthday cake?)

- Difficulty arranging holidays

- Not having the viewpoint of someone of the other sex

- For men – society may be wary of them, especially around children

- For women – safety issues in the house

- People assuming I have lots of free time

- An integrity issue – trying to be the same in public and in private

- Going to places on my own

- Seeing others get married
- Not having children (if that's the case for you)

This is also an interesting list – one that we need to acknowledge and be realistic about. Some of these things are big issues, and things that we will struggle with and find very difficult, but it's worth remembering that the things we each find hard will be different. As you read the list above there will have been some areas that really resonated with you, and others that you didn't identify with at all.

Some things even appeared on both lists! There are things such as the question of money, which some people identified as a positive and others as a negative. For instance, holidays can be more expensive because of single person supplements, but we can save money if we are free to go away during school term time. Shopping can be more expensive because we can't always take advantage of bulk buy special offers (or if we do, we risk wasting food), but obviously there is overall less food to buy!

There are also things on those lists that will be an issue for us at some times and not at others. For me, I know that most of the time I am absolutely fine about being single, but on days when I find it hard, sometimes that's to do with loneliness and having no one to talk to, sometimes it's because I really want to have sex, and sometimes it's because I long to have children. (When it's all three at once, that's a bad day!)

It's also true that some things can be both a positive and a negative, almost at the same time. In summer 2012, when

London was hosting the Olympic and Paralympic Games, I had bought Paralympic tickets with a friend, and we went together one day. I decided that I'd like to also go to the athletics the following day, but my friend had to work, so I went on my own. The brilliant thing about being single in that situation was that I could please myself, make the decision, buy the tickets, travel down to London, and have a great day out, without having to worry about anyone else. The difficult thing was that I had to spend the Friday all by myself. I decided to go anyway, and it was so worth it – I had a fantastic time and I'm so glad I got to experience it. Plus, I bumped into some friends so I didn't spend the whole day on my own after all! I could have decided not to go as I didn't want to do it by myself, but I would have missed out on a really great day. (The amusing postscript to this story is that I asked one of the stewards to take my photograph outside the stadium. He was utterly horrified that I was there on my own, and insisted on being in the photograph with me, while his friend took it. Sometimes we can be quite alright with our singleness, but society isn't!)

My story

Over the past three or four years, since I first spoke at a New Wine conference about singleness, God has brought me on a journey that has been very unexpected. I want to share with you a bit of that journey. I hope that it will be helpful, and will encourage you. Please remember that this is only my story – God has a different story for you, a story all of your own, for you and him to write together.

I mentioned in the introduction that when I was first asked to speak about being single I said no, but that I agreed a year later. During that year I had a very powerful encounter with God in which I felt him speak to me clearly about my singleness in a way that he had never done before. I was at a conference and during the opening worship time I was singing and praising God, and not thinking about anything else except that. Suddenly, I felt God say to me, "You're always going to be single." (What I mean is not that I actually heard a voice, but simply that I had a very strong sense God was telling me something directly and personally.) This was out of the blue, and not especially welcome! So I asked God, if it was really from him, to allow me to forget all about it, and then to tell me again.

That's what he did! I forgot all about it until the next day, when, again during a time of sung worship, I felt him say the same thing. I still didn't really want to hear it. So, at the risk of burying my head in the sand, I asked him to do exactly the same thing as the day before – allow me to forget it, and then tell me again. Amazingly, he did! I completely forgot about it (which really does make me believe it must have been God). The next day (the final day of the conference), during the worship time, I had the same sense of God speaking. This time I began to listen – even my stubbornness only goes so far! I asked God what he was actually saying, and the sense I had was not of him "calling" me to be single, or telling me that I had to be. Rather, it was as if he was simply gently letting me know that this was how my life was going to look.

To be honest, I didn't really know what to make of this. I told a few close friends. They were supportive, of course, but also confused. Although we were all used to sensing God speaking to us about various things, this was something new. What did it mean? Could I be sure? How should I live as a result of it? At first I chose not to tell many people about it, because I still wasn't entirely certain about it all. When I gave talks on being single I didn't mention it, because I didn't know how to describe what had happened. Since then I have told a few more people, and some have suggested that perhaps God was saying something along the lines of: "Will you give up your desire to be married?" They suggested that, if I agreed to do so, he would then promptly send along a husband. I don't go along with that view – I think that smacks too much of the "once your life and your relationship with God are sorted then he'll allow you to get married" viewpoint, which I don't think fits with God's character. Of course we must be careful that our desire for marriage doesn't become an idol, but I don't think that God requires us to be spiritually or emotionally perfect before he drops our perfect partner from the skies!

Hearing from God in that way was wonderful and I am sure that what I heard at that conference was from him and for me, but it still left me unsure as to what would happen next. If a situation arose where there was a possibility for a relationship, would it be alright to pursue that, or not? And even if I did, would anything come from it? As I said earlier, it definitely didn't feel as though God was "calling" me to stay single, so it didn't feel disobedient in pursuing relationships, but I still felt a little uneasy because I wasn't sure what would come of them. (I should say at this point that I was hardly having to beat men off with a stick as they formed a queue to my front door – but it's always good to be prepared!) I continued to ask God to speak to me and show me what to do, and how to live.

Over this past summer, he did just that! I was privileged to be part of a group of women who went to Kenya to visit some great projects run by local Christians. We had the opportunity to speak and minister in a number of different settings, including to Mothers' Union groups. One day, one of the women was speaking about Mary, Jesus' mother, and about the incredible faith and obedience she showed, even at a young age and in the face of such an enormous task. I have always been inspired and challenged by Mary's great faith, and by the words she spoke to the angel after he had dropped his bombshell into her life: "'I am the Lord's servant,' Mary answered. 'May your word to me be fulfilled.'"[4]

I have long tried to follow Mary's example of obedience to God in whatever he asks. I found myself praying as I listened to the talk, saying once again that I wanted my whole life to be lived for God, whatever he asked of me, and whatever that meant. Then someone else stood up and quoted Psalm 37: "Take delight in the Lord, and he will give you the desires of your heart."[5] Most of you who are single will be familiar with this verse. Probably, like me, you will have heard people quote it to you as "proof" that God will send you a marriage partner if that is what you long for. Maybe you will have cried out to God yourself in these words, begging him to grant you this desire. As soon as she said the words, I had a sense of God

183

speaking to me, saying "I know that the desire of your heart is for me, and I love that. I will always give you that desire." I was fairly overwhelmed, but we had a mission trip to carry on with, so it all got stored away in my head and my heart to deal with later.

Once I was home, I took the opportunity to bring all of this to God and to ask him what on earth I was to make of it. What did it mean? What was he saying to me? And what exactly was it that he was asking me to do? I felt at this point that God showed me two different possibilities for how my life could look. One was as a single person – if I went in this direction there would be no husband, and no children, but my life could still be whole and full. There would be more opportunities for ministry this way, and things that wouldn't be possible in the same way with a family, such as overseas travel. The other was to be married. (God didn't expand on *how* he would make this happen but hey, he's God, he can do anything!) If I went in this direction there would be a husband, and children, and all the things that as a little girl I had so longed for – the big wedding, the babies, and the family life. There would still be ministry, of course, for we all have opportunities to serve God, but it would be different, because my time would be committed in other ways.

Please don't see this as me saying that this second path involved a "lesser" ministry – that is absolutely not what I mean. For a start, bringing up children is one of the most important ministries we can ever be involved with, and of course there would still be many other possibilities at church and beyond. Being realistic, though, this second path would look very different in terms of what I could and couldn't commit to, and how much time was available to me. I felt that God told me, very gently and kindly, that the first path was his best for me – the one he had chosen in advance for me to do. It was also very clear, however, that I was able to choose the second path if I wanted to, and that it would be no "less" in his eyes – there would still be joy and blessing that way.

I chose the first path. I chose it immediately, certainly, and wholeheartedly, but, even as I was aware of myself doing so, I was surprised. I thought to myself, "I want to get married and have children – what on earth am I doing?" And yet even as I thought that, I knew there was one thing I wanted more – to love and serve God, and to do his will. It's possible to do both, of course it is, but for me, this was the right path. This *is* the right path.

I've been learning a lot recently about time management, and about planning and prioritizing. When considering the choices we make about how we spend our time and what we agree to do, it is often said that we can only say no to something when we have "a bigger 'yes' burning inside".[6] The argument goes that when we have settled on our absolute priorities, we will find it easier to say no to things that aren't in line with those priorities. That's how it felt in this situation. Because I know what my greatest "yes" is – the desire to love and serve God above all else – I was able to say no to the lesser question of whether I wanted to be married and have children. (I don't mean that was the lesser option, but that it was the lesser *question* – that is, the issue of whether or not I get married is less important than the question of for whom and for what I am living my life.)

So what will my future look like? I have no idea! When I've told friends about my experience, and what I think God has said, some have responded by saying, "Maybe this is for a season, because God has something particular for you to do, and at some time in the future you will get married." Well, maybe that's true, because we never really know what lies ahead – but I am as sure as I can be that actually, this is a choice that I have made for life.

Now please understand me clearly on this. I am not saying that one particular path is intrinsically better or more worthwhile than another. I am not saying that you should make the same choices that I have made. I am not saying that God will speak to you in the way that I believe he has spoken to me. I do, however, believe that God is interested in how you live your life, and in the choices that you make. I believe that he wants to speak to you and guide you. Your story will be different from mine – but it's a story with God at the centre. I know that God wants to talk with you about your story, as he has done with me.

Life to the full

I hope by now I've made it clear that I believe life with Jesus is the best possible life. It just doesn't get any better than this! Or at least, it doesn't get any better on earth. For Christians, we know this isn't our real home – that comes later, when we live forever with God in the new heavens and the new earth. So while we rejoice in and embrace our earthly life, we also look ahead to the future beyond this life.

God wants us to be happy – it isn't wrong to hope for and desire happiness. The way in which God has created us means that we will be most truly happy when we are fully worshipping him and living in line with his will for us. When God is the "bigger yes" burning inside of us, then the other things in life will fall into place.

Here is an awesome statement, from Paul, writing to the church in Corinth: "Where you are right now is God's place for you. Live and obey and love and believe right there. God, not your marital status, defines your life."[7]

It's time for us to embrace our life where we are right now. Our life is a beautiful, precious gift that we have been given and that we can use however we choose. When we choose Jesus, that means choosing "life to the full".[8]

Life with Jesus is about freedom, love, grace, joy, hope, peace, mission, relationship, and adventure. We've only got one life on earth, and it's ours to make the most of – to live, laugh, love, learn, and labour for God. That's real life. That's a God-honouring, Jesus-centred, Spirit-inspired life. That's life to the full, and – whether we're young or old, male or female, married or single – it's the life that God wants for us, the life that glorifies him, the life we were created to live. Bring it on!

Recommended reading

Single Women: Challenge to the Church, Kristin Aune, Paternoster Press, 2002

The Five Love Languages Singles Edition, Gary Chapman, Northfield, 2004

The Single Issue, Al Hsu, IVP, 1997

One: Living the Single Life, Julia Morgan, CWR, 2009

High Heels and Holiness: The Smart Girl's Guide to Living Life Well, Jo Saxton and Sally Breen, Hodder & Stoughton, 2012

Notes

Chapter 1: Wholly single

1. "This Day I Married My Best Friend", author unknown.
2. John 10:10.
3. Genesis 2:24.
4. James Friel, BBC News Magazine Viewpoint "Why are couples so mean to single people?", Wednesday 7 November 2012, http://www.bbc.co.uk/news/magazine-20219349
5. Mariella Frostrup, "The worst thing about being free, is that it generally doesn't last", *The Observer*, Sunday 5 November 2000.
6. Al Hsu, *The Single Issue*, IVP, 1997.
7. 1 Corinthians 7:7.
8. Hebrews 4:15.
9. Philippians 4:11.
10. Psalm 139:13–16, The Message.
11. Genesis 2:18.
12. Colossians 2:9–10.
13. Joshua Harris, *Boy Meets Girl*, Multnomah, 2000.
14. 1 Corinthians 7:34, The Message.
15. Luke 18:29–30.
16. Revelation 21:3–4.
17. Eric and Leslie Ludy, *When God Writes Your Love Story*, Loyal, 1999.
18. Taken from "Great is Thy Faithfulness" by Thomas O. Chisholm. Copyright © 1923, 1951 Hope Publishing Co. Used by permission.

19. Shane Claiborne, "I'm a Fundamentalist, Baby", in *Christianity* magazine, June 2010. Used with permission.

Chapter 2: Living a God-obsessed life in a marriage-obsessed church

1. Genesis 2:18.
2. Isaiah 54:1.
3. Luke 14:26.
4. Matthew 19:11–12.
5. 1 Corinthians 7:7.
6. Al Hsu, *The Single Issue*.
7. Al Hsu, *The Single Issue*.
8. Leslie Ludy, *Sacred Singleness*, Harvest House, 2009.
9. The best resource I have come across for Mothering Sunday is the Grove Booklet "Mothering Sunday" by Em Coley, Grove Worship Series No. 185.
10. Kristin Aune, *Single Women: Challenge to the Church*, Paternoster Press, 2002.
11. Deuteronomy 6:5.
12. Hebrews 11:1.

Chapter 3: Purely single

1. Philippians 4:8.
2. 1 Thessalonians 4:1–8.
3. John 10:10.
4. Quoted in Al Hsu, *The Single Issue*.
5. Romans 12:1–2, The Message.
6. Philippians 4:11–13, The Message.

Chapter 4: Living a God-obsessed life in a sex-obsessed world

1. Romans 12:2.
2. Genesis 1:27–28.
3. Genesis 2:20–24.
4. 2 Corinthians 6:14–15.

5. 1 Corinthians 6:19–20.

6. Kristin Aune, *Single Women: Challenge to the Church*.

7. Philip Wilson, "Sex and the Single Christian", in *The Church of England Newspaper*, September 9 2005.

8. Catherine von Ruhland, "An Unchosen Chastity", *Third Way* magazine, June 2004.

9. Jenny Taylor, "A Wild Constraint", *Third Way* magazine, July 2004.

10. Gary Chapman, *The Five Love Languages Singles Edition*, Northfield, 2004.

11. 2 Corinthians 10:5.

12. Philippians 4:8.

13. Martin Luther, *Works*, Volume 42, p. 73.

14. Thomas Garvey, "The Emotional Trials of the Single Life", in *The Church of England Newspaper*, 2005.

Chapter 5: Single again

1. Beverley Shepherd, *Created as a Woman*, CWR, 2007.

2. Deuteronomy 31:8.

Chapter 6: Living together

1. 1 Corinthians 12:12–27.

Chapter 7: Happily ever after...

1. See *Revelations of Divine Love* by Julian of Norwich.

2. Genesis 2:18.

3. Jo Saxton and Sally Breen, *High Heels and Holiness: The Smart Girl's Guide to Living Life Well*, Hodder & Stoughton, 2012.

4. Luke 1:38.

5. Psalm 37:4.

6. Stephen Covey, *The 7 Habits of Highly Effective People*, Simon & Schuster, 1989.

7. 1 Corinthians 7:17, The Message.

8. John 10:10.